The Water Lies

One Family's Story of Hurricane Katrina

Linda Gannon Mucha

abbott press®

A DIVISION OF WRITER'S DIGEST

The Water Lies
One Family's Story of Hurricane Katrina

Cover Photo: National Oceanic and Atmospheric Administration
Back Cover Photos: Michael Gannon Mucha

Abbott Press books may be ordered through booksellers or by contacting:

Abbott Press
1663 Liberty Drive
Bloomington, IN 47403
www.abbottpress.com
Phone: 1-866-697-5310

ISBN: 978-1-4582-0244-4 (sc)
ISBN: 978-1-4582-0245-1 (e)
ISBN: 978-1-4582-0246-8 (hc)

Library of Congress Control Number: 2012903501

Printed in the United States of America

Abbott Press rev. date: 3/17/2012

Also by Linda Mucha:
Chuckie and Other Gifted Children: Understanding and Advocating for the Gifted Child

For my husband, Ron; our children, Mary Margaret and Michael; and all those angels who sustained us.

Contents

Preface

Many statistics have been published regarding the impact of Hurricane Katrina. When the levies failed New Orleans after Katrina, the near-biblical devastation of New Orleans captivated the world. Less attention was paid to the four hundred thousand people in the three coastal Mississippi counties that bore the brunt of this catastrophic storm on August 29, 2005. *The Water Lies* is one Mississippi coast family's experience as they became part of the statistics collected on Hurricane Katrina.

Katrina, the second Category 5 hurricane of the 2005 hurricane season, impacted over one hundred square miles, consuming the entire Mississippi coast and killing 238 people. The cost of Katrina reached $75 billion in damages, but the damage to the lives it shattered cannot be measured.

Thousands of local residents were irreparably harmed. They were suddenly unemployed, their homes, churches, and schools destroyed. The infrastructure of their cities and communities was damaged or erased completely. Their hospitals were crippled and became much like wartime triage facilities, unable to handle the hundreds of injuries they faced daily.

Tens of thousands of single-family homes were destroyed, leaving images of devastation typically associated with an atomic bomb blast. Katrina's unprecedented thirty-foot storm surge destroyed many homes not located on the coastline or bays. The huge number of displaced people defies the imagination. Families turned to the American Red Cross, the Salvation Army, churches, and other charitable organizations for housing, food, and water. Without these organizations, refugees would have had no help for days, weeks, or even months. Thousands of people—people who had had children and pets, homes and furnishings, cars, trucks, boats, careers, and all the normalcy of life—suddenly faced a new world. In a matter of hours, everything they thought of as theirs was gone. This new world would be hot, humid, muddy, foul, unhealthy, and foreign to their beliefs and experiences, a place where they were nobody and had nothing except a body and mind functioning on only the most perfunctory level.

Over three hundred years of history, culture, and artifacts were destroyed. Streets and neighborhoods were unidentifiable. There were no apartment buildings, businesses, landmarks, or street signs. There were no usable bridges. For miles and miles there was only devastation—buildings, trees, vehicles, and homes with all their contents, mangled together in piles that filled the streets and land that had once been cities and communities. Coastal cities were literally gone.

Katrina was one of the most devastating storms ever to hit the United States. Six years after Katrina, the communities are becoming communities again, but for many, life has changed forever.

Chapter 1 Who We Were

The Water Lies is one family's story of how an act of nature—a hurricane—can change lives forever. It is the story of how one brief force of nature contributed to events and occurrences that are unpredictable and often incomprehensible. It has been six years since Hurricane Katrina arrived on the Mississippi Gulf Coast ... the longest six years of my life and, I believe, of the lives of my family. If any lessons can be learned from reading about our experiences, I hope they teach the value of family bonds, commitment, and facing reality when it clearly cannot be ignored or altered.

We were a family of five on August 29, 2005. Ron and I were the parents of two grown children— Michael and Mary Margaret—and parents-in-law to Scott. Ron was retired from the US Air Force and the Department of Defense. After more than forty years of dedicated work and serving in Southeast Asia during Vietnam, Ron was finally enjoying the retirement he had planned so well.

Ron built two homes during his working years. The first was in Gulfport, Mississippi, in a new subdivision called Bayou Oaks. Our home there was a few blocks from the bayou. It was beautiful and sat deep on an oak-filled lot.

Bayou Oaks home.

Our children were raised there from ages five and eight until their high school and university years. Bayou Oaks was, and is, a small, exclusive, quiet neighborhood, where families are comfortable and secure. Ron planned, saved, and looked forward during the Bayou Oaks years. He wanted to live on the water. He bought and sold two waterfront lots as he accumulated the funds for his real waterfront plan: Back Bay, in Biloxi, Mississippi.

The home Katrina took and the oak tree that fell to the west (right).
It blocked our vehicles from leaving the property and damaging the
house across the street, where we stayed during the storm.

Ron built our second home on a peninsula, Lopez Point on Big Lake, a part of Back Bay. Ron could not have been more pleased with the property. His first accomplishment was a two-hundred-foot pier over marshland to a private beach, where we could fish and crab from the dock. This spot would be our piece of heaven. Two rivers—the Biloxi and the Tchoutacabouffa—feed Big Lake. It has brackish tidal water, because the salt water of Back Bay connects to the Gulf of Mexico, and the fresh water from the two rivers meets the lake right at our dock. Our marshland backyard is a nursery for all types of fish and birds, including shrimp, blue crab, and mullet. (Locally called "Biloxi bacon," mullet are the fish we think of when we sit on the dock of the bay and watch the fish jumpin'.) Our marsh is also home to pelicans, seagulls, red-winged blackbirds, gray herons, and even American eagles. This piece of paradise is where we would retire.

View of the marsh, our backyard.

Ours was a beautiful home nestled under huge live oaks dripping with Spanish moss, and no man ever planned longer or worked harder to build his home than Ron did. He reminded me of the Peter character in *Peter and the Wolf* as he walked along his beach with a piece of driftwood for a staff, exploring every inch of the waterline. Ron could walk among nature for hours, enjoying the gifts God has given our earth. On occasion, he would become overwhelmed by the beauty of it all. Sometimes he would run down our pier, shed his swimsuit, and jump right into the bay, smiling and hooting. At times like those, Ron wasn't sixty years old—he was more like sixteen!

Ron always believed he was blessed and needed to be a blessing for others. He served and supported Goodwill Industries and the Salvation Army. He was particularly dedicated to the Mississippi Special Olympics, serving as its president and as a member of its executive board. Most important to Ron was serving the athletes. Ron loved sailing and owned a couple of sailboats over the years. While sailing one evening, he shared with me that he wanted to start a sailing event for the Special Olympians. I had reservations, because sailing can be a dangerous sport. Ron was determined, however, and he went about getting Hobie Cats donated and securing the Ocean Springs Yacht Club for the events. Because of its wide, shallow beach, it was a perfect location to practice and host regattas. Before long, Ron had established his sailing team with all the rights and privileges afforded by the National Special Olympics. He established an annual Southeastern regatta competition, and his team competed at the national events. Eventually, he took the team to Ireland for international competition, where one of his sailors won the silver medal and another won the gold. His sailors loved him as much as he loved them and the water.

I hope you are getting a fairly good picture of Ron: wonderful father and family man; well educated, with a bachelor's degree from Rutgers and a master's from Pepperdine; and a Eucharistic minister at Nativity Cathedral. Ron never met a person he wouldn't help if he or she needed him. And Ron didn't know how to frown—he had a ready smile and handshake. Throughout Ron's military career, he traveled the world. He made friends everywhere he lived and kept up with many of them. Whether he was Boy Scout leader or PTA president, Ron gave abundantly of himself, and blessings were abundant for him.

I was never as active as Ron. I love to read and write. I love school. Educational theory and gifted children intrigue me. As a young wife, I wanted all the good things in life a small-town southern girl would want. I wanted a university teaching degree so I could teach children; I wanted to fall in love and have children of my own. I wanted a home near my mother and other family in Gulfport, I wanted my church and friends, and I wanted to travel some. Ron provided all those things and more.

We met on a blind date when I was a senior in college and Ron was about to leave for Vietnam. Ours was a truly perfect courtship. The only time we were apart was when he left for Southeast Asia, and I finished my schooling as an engaged, busy young woman, waiting for her future husband to return home. After we married, we lived in California, where Mary Margaret was born, and I had my first teaching experience. Our next assignment was Florida, where Michael was born. Then we returned to Gulfport, where Ron finished his air force career at Keesler Air Force Base.

We had the same hills to climb that most young couples have, but our life together never lost the love we felt the day we married. It grew stronger, and for me, life was as good as it could get. I had everything I ever wanted. Once begun, my teaching career continued uninterrupted for twenty-six years. I earned a master's and specialist degrees and a doctorate while working, raising kids, and enjoying my mother, brothers, sisters, children, and husband. Life was full, often challenging, but never unhappy.

We lost Ron's mom and dad, my mother, and one of my sisters over the years. I had lost my father when I was four years old. So, my family was and is very important to me. Mine is a very close family, and Ron and I raised our little family to be a close and an integral part of it. We have roots—a treasured part of life in the South. Traditions are important, and our children were steeped in family and tradition.

Our family gatherings were, and are, frequent. Birthdays, graduations, and holidays are all celebrations when we cook, eat, laugh, and simply enjoy having each other. When one of us suffers, we all suffer. When one of us is blessed, we all are blessed. Parties at our home on the bay were and continue to be a wonderful part of our lives. We have boiled so many shrimp that it's a wonder there are shrimp left to buy! We enjoy seafood gumbo and boiled blue crabs. When the tugboats bring the coal barges by our backyard, with seagulls laughing at their catch from the furled waves, and a big orange sun is setting on the horizon, there are no words to express how blessed we feel. While it broke my heart to leave our home in Bayou Oaks, where we raised our children, Ron's choice of living on the bay soon filled my heart with the wonder of the water and Mother Nature. We are home there.

Our daughter, Mary Margaret, is a beautiful, loving, gifted young woman. She finished college, became a teacher, and earned her master's degree—sailing with us all the while. Her college life was filled with academic honors and leadership positions in her sorority and at the university. When she graduated she had time for a young sailing friend of Ron's. They had a yearlong courtship that ended in a lovely, traditional wedding at our church, the diocesan cathedral. She was a stunning bride, and her husband was a most handsome groom. When Ron walked her down the aisle of the cathedral, my heart was filled with love and pride and gratitude that we were so blessed.

Our son-in-law, Scott, is an airline pilot, and his career took them first to Colorado and then to Washington, DC. The bonds we held so dearly remained strong, and we visited one another often. We sailed the Potomac with them; they sailed the Mississippi coast with us.

Our son, Michael, a gifted and handsome young man, attended college on scholarships and graduated a year early with a degree in chemistry. He became an air force officer, like his father before him. We traveled to Washington state to visit him and then to his next station in Delaware, where we enjoyed the blue crabs the area waters provided. Michael visited with us and Mary Margaret as often as his military life would allow. He served in the Iraq War, which caused us much worry, and our faith was strengthened when he returned home without injury. Later, when a training injury prevented his second tour in Iraq, we thanked God for the favor. Michael currently teaches chemistry at a local high school.

After Hurricane Katrina, Michael married Cecily, a precious young woman, an artist, who occupies a big part of our hearts. (You will learn why she is so special to us a little later.) They were married in a traditional ceremony in the same cathedral where our daughter married. Cecily was a beautiful bride, and Michael was a handsome groom. It was a fairy-tale wedding we all cherished.

So there you have a brief description of who we were before life as we knew it changed—swiftly and dramatically. Little did we know how fleeting our happy days would be.

It's fortunate that we can't know the future; if we did, it could destroy the beauty of our present and even taint the happiness of our past. Not knowing whether the light at the end of the tunnel is the sun or a train is a good thing. Living in the now is the most important living we can do. Life provides no guarantees, regardless of how well we plan. Life only provides the moment we have, which can be plenty if we fill that moment with love and purpose. Remember that old saying, "It's not nice to fool Mother Nature?" I have a better one: "It's not nice to doubt Mother Nature." On August 29, 2005, and the days that preceded it, Ron doubted Mother Nature.

But I'm getting ahead of my story.

When we rang in 2005, we did it with a big celebration at our home. I had just retired, and Ron and I were planning a long-awaited visit to Rome in March. With family home from all over the country and Europe, we ate, drank, sang, and danced to usher in the New Year. We were glad to be all together, healthy and happy to see each other. Nieces brought their new babies and growing youngsters. We older folks thought we looked pretty good for our ages, and we were glad we could still "cut a rug" as we did in the old days. All the catching-up chatter and the delightful accents of our New Orleans friends and relatives made the evening festive. Our little grand-dog daughter, a maltipoo named Bitsy Belle, stole the show that evening. Having been an expensive and very special puppy—Mary Margaret had waited a year to get her—we knew Bitsy Belle would demonstrate impeccable manners at our gala affair. We were all taken aback when she nuzzled her way into the trash can, emerged with boiled shrimp hulls stuck to her white curls, and then ran out the front door and leaped across our neighbors' lawns like Santa's reindeer in flight. (We still tease our daughter about her very expensive, very embarrassing little dog!) Regardless, we knew 2005 would be a wonderful year. Half of it was.

Retirement life was just what Ron and I needed. In the mornings we slept late and then sat on the back balcony overlooking the early tides, where we read the newspaper and listened to the coast birds greet us. We sailed whenever we liked, ate whenever we were hungry, soaked and drank wine in the hot tub, and felt like newlyweds again. March arrived very quickly, and we were so ready for Rome.

When the children were young, Ron and I took them to Brussels and then by train to Paris. It was a wonderful experience for us all, but as parents, it was somewhat stressful. We, or at least I, felt terribly responsible for the kids' every move. I doubt any Belgian or Frenchman wanted to kidnap either of my children, but I was in the protective mode of a mother bear. Even the flights from New York to London and back were trials for me, relieved only by my mantra of the rosary, which I prayed nonstop, round-trip. My grandmother had given me my rosary when I made my first communion at age six, and I kept it in my jacket pocket as I prayed.

This trip to Rome would not be stressful at all. We had done our jobs as parents, and this would be our time, the honeymoon we never had. Until then, all our vacations had been for the kids. We had traveled to the Northeast to visit Ron's relatives, to Disney World, to the Smoky Mountains and Florida's beaches, but always with the kids and with an agenda. This vacation was for us. We were as free as the seagulls and pelicans we left behind at home.

Our hotel in Rome was perfect. To reach our room, we exited a hotel hallway onto a private terra-cotta terrace furnished with mosaic-tiled tables and cushioned, high-backed chairs. Flower-covered vines grew from huge pots up trellises and onto the stone walls of the hotel. The terrace itself was surrounded by a four-foot stone wall, and on the terrace were potted lemon trees with fruit hanging on them, ready to pick. Our room had shuttered windows that opened to allow a cool breeze to flow through the sitting area; the scent of lemons and flowers permeated our curtains and bed linens.

We never turned on the television, although the BBC would have given us the news of the day. Instead, we spent our days walking Rome, seeing the tourist haunts like Trevi Fountain and the Spanish Steps. We ate at fine restaurants and trattorias until we found a special little restaurant with wonderful waiters who gave us after-dinner liqueurs and dessert and would not accept payment for any of their treats. Several times we returned there, to our corner table by a window. We bought

Italian jewelry that we agreed would be our anniversary, birthday, and Christmas presents for several years. We ate gelato at least twice a day and laughed aloud at how blessed we were to be in Rome without a phone or anyone who knew us. We danced to no music on our little terrace and slept like babies.

Our visit to the Vatican was a powerful experience for both of us. Pope John Paul II was in the hospital when we arrived in Rome and returned home just after we visited St. Peter's Basilica. It was sad to see the pope's window, from where he blessed the faithful, dark; we knew he wouldn't live much longer. Years earlier we had taken the kids to New Orleans for the pope's visit and his Mass there. He was so alive then, and I felt such a spiritual connection with him. Now, standing in the Vatican, I realized he had accomplished his work in this life. Soon, his successor would be determined in the very room where I stood. This place, its art, and the burial places of earlier popes were all part of my religious tradition. I knew I would treasure this visit for the rest of my life.

Ron knew the impact the experience had on me. When we returned to Rome, we spent most of the evening just walking and talking about our day. Ron shared anecdotes from his time in Rome before we met and told me funny stories about parking his BMW motorcycle inside the hotel where he stayed. He took me there, and the hotel was just as he described it, right down to the column where he had chained his BMW. I left Rome with a happy heart, a strong faith, and a precious husband who had made this vacation one of the best times of our marriage.

We returned home with memories to treasure, grateful to sleep in our own bed. I vowed to redecorate the house in my new-found free time. I wanted lots of the reds and yellows I loved so much in Italy, and I intended to buy new dinnerware to remind me of our visit there. I wanted lemon liqueur and olives and cheeses and red wine with every meal. For days after our return home, I "mamma-mia-ed" and "ciao-ed" everyone. It was wonderful fun, and the memories still make me smile.

Although I had retired, I had contracted to consult in several southeastern states. So shortly after we returned from Rome, I spent some time working with a school district in Tennessee, preparing for trainings and completing reports. Ron, meanwhile, was preparing his sailors and sailboats for the upcoming regatta in the Mississippi Special Olympics.

Our lives were falling into a normalcy that felt really good. We sailed during the days and enjoyed the hot tub in the evenings. In June, Mary Margaret and Bitsy Belle came for a visit that included day trips to New Orleans and weathering a tropical storm.

During the regatta, an afternoon thunderstorm developed on one of the barrier islands. When they saw lightning in the distance, Ron and others worked quickly to get all the athletes out of the water. I was on my way to the regatta, talking with my sister on my cell phone, when I noted menacing clouds on the water's horizon and witnessed a very impressive lightning strike. I told my sister I hoped the athletes were out of the water.

View of the Special Olympics Regatta from the Ocean Springs Yacht Club.

When I arrived at the Ocean Springs Yacht Club, there was an ambulance there with lights flashing. Ron and another man had been struck by lightning. Ron had been pulling a Hobie Cat onto the shore by the guideline when he was struck; it knocked him back into the water, but he was able to reach the sand. The other man was farther behind Ron, deeper in the water. Others helped him to shore, and an ambulance took him to the hospital. I talked with Ron and insisted that he go to the hospital as well. After being examined in the emergency room, Ron was released with congratulations; he'd been very fortunate. The other person was admitted and then released a few days later. It was a harrowing experience for everyone.

A few days after the regatta, Ron and I flew to Virginia to visit our daughter and son-in-law. During the flight I noticed that Ron's face had turned bright red and appeared swollen. Once we landed, it returned to normal. I have often wondered if that change was related to the lightning strike, and if the lightning strike contributed to Ron's stroke two months later.

Other than that temporary change in Ron's appearance, he seemed fine. We had many plans for that summer, and the Virginia trip was just the beginning. Next we would celebrate my birthday in New Orleans, and then we would travel to Jackson, Mississippi, for another Special Olympics event.

New Orleans was our favorite place to visit. One of the biggest events in the U.S. is the tradition of Mardi Gras in New Orleans. Mardi Gras is a time of special parties and parades filled with marching bands and huge floats from which masked riders throw beads and trinkets to thousands of parade goers. To participate on the floats, one must be a member of a Krewe. This is a group of revelers who meet during the year, give and attend parties, and purchase the Mardi Graw throws they sail from the floats to the crowds. I was a member in the Mardi Gras Krewe of Iris, and Ron was a member of the Krewe of Thoth. For many years we spent Mardi Gras at a French Quarter condominium, part of the Chateau on St. Philip Street. We had become friends with the people at the Chateau, and so we stayed there for a few days for my August birthday. New Orleans is hot and humid in August, but so is the Mississippi coast. For some reason, the music and pure fun of New Orleans make the climate acceptable.

In Jackson we attended an auction benefiting the Mississippi Special Olympics. After several glasses of wine, I fell in love with a very large oil painting entitled *The Water Never Lies*. Not to be outbid,

I continued to raise my paddle until that lovely piece of art was mine. I was delighted with my purchase but had no idea where it would hang. We returned home with many treasures from a silent auction, as well. Between the "must haves" from our New Orleans trip and the "absolutely must haves" from Jackson, our den took on the look of a department store. This problem would not last long.

Chapter 2 Hurricane Warning

I teach at a university whose main campus is about eighty minutes north of Biloxi, and I had a class there on Saturday, August 27. I was aware of a storm brewing in the Gulf, but as I drove to the university, my mind was on what I would cover that day in class and where I would put the various purchases I had made in New Orleans and Jackson. The weather was lovely. Jimmy Buffett kept the mood light, and I pushed that nagging worry about the storm as far away as I could. While I was in class, Ron had decided to secure the Special Olympics' sailboats. He spent his day on that project.

Class went well; I particularly enjoyed this course and the graduate students in the class. It was a fast-paced morning, and around noon a couple of students suggested we leave early because of the impending weather. I didn't take them seriously, as the storm was a good way out and appeared to be headed for east Texas or west Louisiana. But after lunch, when university workers showed up and began covering the computers with plastic, it got my attention and I dismissed class. Students hurriedly helped me pack their projects in the trunk and backseat of my car. Then they wished me well, warned me to be careful, and said they would pray I would get home safely. I thanked them, wondering at their high level of concern for me. There was plenty of time before the storm could threaten us, and I believed it was projected to make landfall far away to our west.

I did, however, trade the Jimmy Buffett CD for the radio as I drove back to the coast—and I quickly realized how much the situation had changed. The Mississippi coast was now a projected path of the hurricane, as was New Orleans, seventy miles to our west. I prayed

13

that we would take the storm rather than New Orleans; I knew that the city I loved so much couldn't stand a direct hit. Note to self: be careful what you pray for.

When I reached the coast, I filled my tank with gas, went to the grocery store, and bought a week's supply of staples—nonperishable food, water, batteries, bleach, and all the other items I knew we'd need during and after a hurricane. When I arrived home, I was surprised to find our son there. Michael was stationed in Montgomery, Alabama, at Maxwell Air Force Base, where he taught at Air University. But here he was, securing all our outdoor furniture and plants. Ron had finished securing the Special Olympics' sailboats and equipment and had also purchased two generators and two air conditioners. We were right on track, I thought, preparing for the storm just as I had done from the time I was a child. I assumed that Ron and I would follow Michael back to his home in Prattville, Alabama, and stay there until the storm was over. After an unpleasant conversation with Ron, however, I realized that I would have to force him into evacuating.

That Saturday evening while Ron slept, Michael and I continued to prepare, listening to the hurricane warnings and discussing how we could convince Ron that we had to evacuate. The next morning we realized we were not alone in our conviction. Our daughter, her husband, and several of their friends called Ron repeatedly, trying to persuade him to leave, as did my brothers and sister, who let us know where they were going and how we could get in touch with them. My family tried nonstop to impress upon me the dangers we would face if we stayed, but they were unable to talk with Ron after mid-morning, when he left for the marina to help other boaters ready their boats. He then began the slow process of motoring our sailboat from the marina across Back Bay and Big Lake, past our dock, and on up the river to a place the locals call "Hurricane Hole."

Biloxi has two schooner ships, the *Secoule* and the *Swetman*. Coastians love and revere these replicas of old wooden schooners. When hurricanes threaten, the ships are moored in Hurricane Hole, an inlet up the river that affords them safety. From their procession to Hurricane Hole, Ron called me on his cell to come to the dock and wave them on their way. For a moment, I thought he had surely lost his mind. Michael and I were busy boarding up the entire back of the house, which was exposed to the south and would bear the brunt of the hurricane-force winds. The thought that I should be on the dock, waving to Ron, seemed surreal. As I saw him nearing, however, I went down and waved and yelled for him to be careful.

Michael and I worked until dark, when he went to retrieve Ron from the riverbank near where our sailboat was moored. After Katrina, our sailboat would be found lodged in a tree, thirty feet above the water.

Michael drove Ron to the marina to collect his truck, arriving back at home before Ron did. Michael warned me that, based on his conversation with Ron, I would not be able to convince him to leave that evening. I would have to make a choice: go to Prattville without Ron and be safe, or remain at home with him and risk both our lives. I understood that there would be no other options. When Ron returned home, his manner and statements confirmed our son's prediction.

As Michael pulled out of the driveway, I felt more alone than I had ever felt in my life. Our neighbors to the west of us were gone; their neighbor at the tip of Lopez Point was gone, too. The family across the street seemed to be at home. Their house faced ours and backed up to the river. A few men in houses east of us stayed, but they had sent their wives and children out of the area. A couple of families on Lopez Point stayed. I discovered who was still on the point after the hurricane passed the next day.

It was very quiet in our home that Sunday night. Ron and I hardly spoke to each other. He was pouting because he felt that all of Biloxi would have to flood for us to be in danger. He knew the quality of the house he had built, and he knew how a fierce hurricane behaves. He and I were dating in 1969 when Hurricane Camille destroyed the coast; he had bagged dead bodies in Pass Christian after that storm. He sincerely believed that Katrina, as powerful as it was predicted to be, would not surpass Camille—and he could handle Camille. He thought I should trust his judgment.

I was not pouting; I was frightened. I knew we were not safe. I remembered my aunt and uncle who lived on the beach road, Highway 90, during Camille. They spent hours straddling a windowsill, fending off kitchen appliances, lumber, house framing, and tidal waves. They were fortunate to have lived through that night, and the memories they shared were horrific. I had seen the videos of people after Camille, embracing each other in shock; they had lost everything they owned. I didn't want those memories. I didn't want to fight for my life, or Ron's, in raging waters, holding fast to some storm-torn tree. I knew these events could be in store for me, and I did not want them. It seemed so much easier to leave and be safe. I could handle anything I might find when I returned, but at least I would not be a part of the nightmare I knew others had endured.

I expressed all this to Ron, and more. But he was firm in his belief that we would be fine, and that should the house take a hit, he needed to be there to prevent excessive damage. I had no argument that could dissuade Ron from his conviction that I was wrong and he was right.

With no apparent options, I began the rituals I had learned as a child and practiced all my adult life when hurricanes threatened: I burned blessed candles, prayed the rosary, and burned palms saved from Palm Sunday Mass and crossed each of us with its ashes. I showered, dressed for the next day, and waited.

All evening our children continued to call, pleading with us to go to a local shelter, at least. Their good advice fell on deaf ears; Ron would not leave, and I would not leave him. We drank coffee and watched the local news, hearing over and over how critical it was that everyone in our area evacuate. Recorded phone calls from the governor came frequently with the same warnings, as they had for two days. Still, we sat and waited.

When sunrise came and the winds picked up, I was as awake as I have ever been. I thought I could feel the house vibrating ever so slightly. Ron assured me that it was just my imagination and advised me to read my book. I thought he must be in a state of denial, and I began to realize that I would eventually have to leave him alone in the house. Where I would go at such a late time I wasn't sure. I just became aware that I would leave him and not be there for him when he needed me. My guilt at this realization was so powerful that even today, six years later, I feel its weight on my heart.

I sat in my study for a while, looking at the vast library I had acquired, and thought of the long hours I'd spent there working on my doctorate. I cried at the thought of leaving the books that had become such a part of me. I had first editions, signed copies of books written by the giants on whose shoulders I stood throughout my career and my studies. I knew, deep down, that I would never see those books again. They were like irreplaceable friends. I studied a signed photograph of Eudora Welty and thought how disappointed she would be to know I did not protect such an artifact. I leafed through signed copies of John Grisham first editions and signed books by Joseph Renzulli. Then, as I was leaving the study, I stopped at a framed rubbing my sister had done for me of Ralph Waldo Emerson's tombstone. I was about to apologize for not being able to protect all of them when the telephone rang, bringing me back to the critical nature of time.

When I answered, I recognized the voice of my neighbor to the west who had left the area. As we talked, I made a decision: I told her I was going to the neighbor's house across the street. When we hung up, I felt the walls of the study to see if I really felt a vibration. I knew it was real, and I dialed my neighbors to see if they were home. The phone just rang. I learned later that they were using the phone line to monitor the storm on the Internet.

I hung up the phone when Ron came into the study. I turned to him, and in a calm, almost prophetic voice that did not seem to come from me, I told him I wasn't wrong. My head and teeth hurt, the house was vibrating, and I was leaving. I told him I was going to start at the house across the street and continue up the street until I found someone who was home. When he started to speak, I interrupted him. Whatever he had to say was no longer a consideration. I told him that while I loved him and had promised to be with him through good and bad, I had never promised I would die for him. They were harsh words, and I'm so grateful that I don't have to live with them without him.

I left Ron in the study and went to our bedroom. I put on my rain jacket, found the plastic bag of jewelry that I had taken to Jackson with me the week before, picked up my purse and another plastic bag filled with important papers, and started for the side door that we had left un-boarded. Ron followed behind, putting on his jacket. He was talking, but I don't remember what he said. When I opened the door, the rain was horizontal, pelting my left side from the west. I had to stoop to walk. Ron, being much stronger than I was, could stand and actually reached our neighbor's house before I did. They were home and welcomed us.

Once we were inside, Ron reiterated his belief that all of Biloxi would have to flood for us to be in danger. I said that I'd felt our house vibrate and I thought it just might lift up. Everyone assured me this would not happen, and I said I supposed I was overreacting and should go back home. Our neighbors, however, insisted we stay with them, since they had an uninterrupted power system. They fixed us coffee, and we settled in for the storm.

I was so grateful for the opportunity to stay with our neighbors. My comment about going back home was a feeble attempt to sound brave and in control, but inside I was in a state of panic. It is still difficult for me to put the fear I felt into words. True fear isn't just mental, it is physical as well. Fear made me want to forget all the normal, acceptable behaviors by which we live. I wanted to scream and cry and tell everyone that they were foolish and our lives would not be spared. I wanted to run from Lopez Point as fast as I could, and I wanted to physically crawl out of my skin. I was in a state of mental and physical torment that no one would even consider the reasoning that seemed so clear to me. I had been raised to be respectful and considerate of others, and I felt I could very well pay for that training with my life.

I thought of my children being without me and not understanding why I would risk my life. They knew that I was seasoned in hurricanes and should have been stronger in my convictions, leaving Ron, the house, and all of it behind. They wouldn't comprehend why I hadn't chosen to live and be there for them.

My brothers and sister knew I was intelligent; they knew I understood that staying was wrong on so many levels. They had to be confused by my weakness, by my choice to ignore the reality of my situation. They expected more of me than to make such illogical, irresponsible choices with my life. My poor decision would negatively impact them, too.

These thoughts raced through my mind, my very being, like an unrelenting burst of energy that wanted to explode. Yet, somehow, I showed none of what I was feeling. I forced an exterior calmness, the demeanor of a wavering, unsure person willing to accept what was being said to me. But I was frustrated and angry at my own behavior, and even now, six years later, the very memory causes a wave of nausea that makes me consciously compartmentalize those feelings.

Just putting these words on paper brings me a step closer to dealing with those pent-up emotions. While I'm writing this story in part for others to know they are not alone in their self-incrimination for poor decisions, I'm also writing in order to release these thoughts and feelings, to tell myself that I'm okay and that this self-imposed guilt will fade.

Chapter 3 Katrina Arrives

Even before I finished my coffee, my niece called me on my cell phone, very concerned that we hadn't evacuated. She was relieved to learn that we were not alone, so, reassured that we were with neighbors, she hung up. Shortly afterward, I heard an arrhythmic popping sound—it popped, then stopped, then popped some more. I asked my neighbor if it could be the power lines breaking. He reminded me that our power lines were underground. Then Ron came into the breakfast area with a look of anxiety and fear that told me I'd need to steady myself.

His voice was low and guttural, with a sense of despair I don't think I had heard from him before that moment. He said just a few words, but their tone screamed, "I was wrong—oh my God! How can I fix this?" Apparently, the popping sounds I'd heard had been our garage roof ripping away from the main roof of our house.

Ron always fixed everything. He embraced the role of provider, protector, and pastor. He lived for his family and loved us with his whole heart. I knew the pain he felt; that very moment I absorbed it and felt it, too. I think he saw that I understood his state of mind. When we looked at each other, I just nodded. Who was this strong person I was pretending to be? I wanted to grab Ron with both arms and just hold him, but I didn't. I simply nodded that I understood.

I went to the front door and saw that our garage roof was in our front yard.

When it was built, the garage had a lot of space above the ceiling, and there was a narrow walkway from the garage roof into the roof of the main house. I used to tease our kids that someday our teenage grandchildren would sneak through that walkway to the garage attic, open the dormer that overlooked the bay, and secretly smoke cigarettes. I told them that I would monitor that window and bust them as soon as a smoke signal appeared. We laughed many times at the thought of this.

When Ron and I were newly married, we went to Mexico and I purchased a scary ceramic skull with a rat on its temple. I bought it as a Halloween decoration. Later I would tell the kids I intended to place it in that secret garage attic so it would scare the grandchildren if they ventured there. Actually, we planned to use that area for storage if we needed it, and secondarily to entertain our grandchildren.

Now I looked out my neighbor's front door at the dormer that used to face the bay. It was still affixed to the roof but fighting against the wind, torn and twisted so that now it faced me. I know that inanimate objects cannot communicate, but that dormer stared at me and told me there would be no future … no need for extra storage, no grandkids to scare or catch puffing away. Our lives as we planned them and hoped and prayed for them to be were just fantasy. This was reality, that dormer said. And the reality was that this was the beginning of the end.

Our car and truck, the newly purchased air conditioners and generators, the outdoor furniture, the plants, the grill, and all the other items Michael and I had so precisely packed in our garage, now sat in a torrent of rain and howling wind. The vehicles would not help us escape; the generators and air conditioners would not sustain us after the storm. All our efforts to protect our belongings from the elements and all our plans for living after the storm were just more fantasies. With defeated calm, I accepted that we had wasted our energy and hope pretending we could prepare for Katrina. We hadn't faced reality, and now the only way to face the impending disaster was to meet it head-on.

The garage was detached except where its roof had been tied to the bayside roof of our house. The small walkway that had led from the house to the garage attic was now gone, and I realized that losing that connection compromised the integrity of the house roof; severe damage would result. Still, I wasn't willing to accept the inevitable destruction of our home. I silently prayed that the storm would pass quickly and that any damage would not reach the study at the front of the house. I suppose I pleaded rather than prayed. A new mantra—*Please, God, spare my study, spare my books, no one but You knows how much I love them. Please, save my study*—roared through my thoughts, as loud as the battering wind.

When the wind forced our neighbor's front door shut, it began to dawn on me that we, too, were in serious danger, even across the street. I reached into my pants pocket for my rosary, and it wasn't there; I had left it on my bedside table. I felt such a loss. I had prayed on that rosary for more than fifty years, I thought, and now, when I needed the comfort of its worn crystals, they had been left behind, with all those plans for the future.

I sat alone in the breakfast area and quietly began to recite the rosary on my fingers, trying to focus on my prayers. The sound of the wind was so strong that in my mind I yelled the words; I don't even recall what I prayed for. I just wanted desperately to replace the sound of that vicious, unrelenting wind. Ron interrupted me to say that he could see light when he looked through the arched glass above the French doors on our front porch. If he saw light coming through our house, that meant the windows on the bay side of the house had lost the boards protecting them. This time, I did not nod, but grabbed his arm and said, "Oh my sweet Jesus! Ron, oh, my God, Ron." My face must have told him I needed him to say that it would be over soon, that it would all be okay, because he took his gaze from me to the floor and kept it there a long moment.

I decided that Ron must be wrong. I would look at our house, and then I'd be able to tell him he had simply seen a glare of some sort.

I went to look and determined that the back of the house, or at least the back windows, were indeed compromised. What a nebulous word, *compromised*—I wanted to bargain this reality away, to logically negotiate the reality that was bearing down on me. I told myself that yes, the roof had lifted off the garage, and that probably ripped some roofing off the house, which in turn caused the protective boarding to catch a gust of wind. Then, I supposed, some of those boards covering the back windows came loose and allowed light to come through to the front of the house. If this was true, it didn't mean the house was irreparable, that everything would be lost. It simply meant that if the windows broke, we would have to deal with water damage. Meanwhile my innermost voice was screaming that I had to wake up and *do* something—but what? I couldn't compromise or negotiate the fact that I was experiencing an end to life as I knew it, planned it, and wanted it to be.

In a slow-motion, almost robotic state, I returned to my spot in the breakfast area and continued my prayers. There was nothing else I could do. I didn't ask anything particular from God or even give thanks that I wasn't in our home. I gave up trying to pray louder than Katrina roared. I think I was trying to establish some compartments in which I could store these experiences and close the door on them— the way I've always dealt with things I cannot change.

Suddenly, Ron came into the room and fell into the chair across the table from me. His fists were balled, and he was rocking back and forth, repeating, "It's gone. It's all gone." I didn't go to him. I went to the front of the house and asked my neighbor what had happened. He tried his best to deter me from looking, but when I pleaded, he cracked the door.

Our home was gone. Water covered the place where it used to be, the crashing waves moving lumber and debris the way a washing machine moves clothes. Behind the water, everything was white—a very bright white. There might have been objects in the white, but now I can only recall how shocked I was that there was no dark storm cloud over the bay. Instead it was as bright a white as the clouds below an airliner at thirty thousand feet. It wasn't puffy like clouds, however; it was more like a sheet. I also saw that the huge live oak in our front yard had fallen to the west, crossing our driveway and our neighbor's. I felt a sense of dread, knowing that tree was down.

That oak had been the tallest tree on the point. Every fall, a bald eagle would perch on its topmost branches and stay for the longest time, surveying the bay—planning his next meal, I assumed. Ron had taken several pictures of the eagle over the years. We learned that eagles nested across the bay to the west in an area called Eagle Point. Now the eagle's resting place was gone forever, just as ours was.

The sound of the storm and the pressure of the wind on my face and body were ferocious, but still I held onto the door, no longer lost in thought but becoming aware of the elements of this storm. I was trying to imprint the image of the inconceivable on my memory. Unfortunately, I was successful. In that split second, I went from the secure wife, mom, and professor who lived on South Shore Drive to a confused, defeated, frightened, homeless, helpless, horrified woman. I was numb.

With numbness comes a compelling lethargy that says it's okay to succumb, it's wise to wish no more. Numbness is very calming—it allowed me not to care about what was happening. It prevented me from decision making or problem solving. I had no control; I could exhale. If I could maintain that sensation of disconnection from anything or anyone, I could come through all this. I tried not to think, but just to be.

We had to close the door quickly because of the wind and the air pressure. But in the few seconds that I stood there, I realized that I was still alive—we were all still alive. I don't remember thinking much about our home being gone. I just returned to the breakfast area and studied Ron for a few moments. He had not changed his position or his rocking motion. I remember thinking that he was too emotional and wasn't capable of calming himself. I wondered why he couldn't just settle down—our home was gone, and now we had to relax about it. It was a surreal experience, like when people describe hovering above the operating room table, watching their own surgery. I felt that detachment looking at Ron. I couldn't help him. It was too late. We had stayed and we were living the nightmares I had so wanted to avoid. Here we were, and here we would remain.

My neighbor told me that we could handle a storm, but we couldn't handle a heart attack. I needed to calm Ron.

Ron had had a heart attack eight years earlier. He had stents put in the clogged arteries that caused it and had been fine since then. Not knowing what to do, I gave Ron two shots of bourbon from the bar and had a shot of tequila myself. I couldn't feel any effect, so I doubted the liquor would help him, either. I then tried calmly explaining that our home was insured—the important thing, I said, was that we were alive. I told him we would rebuild and everything would be fine. I was continuing to reassure him when our neighbor came in and said we needed to move upstairs because the water was rising quickly.

We went to a second-floor bedroom on the east side of the house. I moved to the window that faced east and a overlooked a vacant lot. When I felt the window, there was the same vibration I'd felt in the walls of what used to be my home. I knew our situation was getting worse. From the window I could see the bay, white-capped and turbulent, rushing across the vacant lot. It carried boats and a truck and all sorts of lumber and trees. The power of the wind, rain, and relentlessly surging water warned me that we could, and probably would, die that day.

I consciously wanted to live. I wanted to leave Lopez Point with Ron and never look back. I wanted to beat Katrina at her own game. I knew I was smart and could adjust to whatever this storm did; I just had to shed my numbness and sense of defeat. I had to gather my wits and face the reality of the situation. I had to garner some willpower and self-control.

Suddenly, in the midst of the raging water and torrential winds, I decided I needed to contact our daughter and tell her we were okay and that I was so sorry, but we had lost our home—their home, the place where they could always return. That call would be my first step in making this experience real: I had to face it, accept it, and begin to deal with it.

To my surprise, the phone had a dial tone, and I called Mary Margaret's home number, expecting her to be at work. I had rehearsed the message I would leave and planned how calm and at ease my voice would be. When she answered, I was shocked. I asked why she was home and not in her classroom. She said she was too upset; everyone at school was watching the storm on television, and the principal had sent her home with a colleague who would stay with her until Scott returned from a flight that evening. I told her that we were with neighbors, we were fine, but the house was gone, and that I was so sorry to have to tell her that. Crying, she asked if we were going to die. That startled me. I couldn't imagine my child being in such a state that she would be thinking that. It was evident that she had faced the reality of our situation long before I had.

I assured Mary Margaret that if there were no more tornados, we would be fine, and I asked her to contact her brother and let him know we were okay. Then the phone line died, and there was silence.

I don't know why I thought we were in the midst of tornados. With everything so unsettled and unnatural, I suppose that is how my mind identified the environment. I learned later that when the phone line died, our daughter collapsed. She had no way of knowing what had happened, and she would not know for days whether we lived or died. She was left in a limbo of panic and depression, experiencing the very nightmare I so wanted her to avoid. Our neighbor's son and his wife and young son, about four years old, were also staying at the house, and I realized how much danger the young boy would be in if things got much worse. He was in an upstairs bedroom, watching movies and cartoons on a DVD player, so I went in and visited with him for a little while. I thought it would be important for him to be comfortable with me if I had to help him in a bad situation later. After our visit, as I walked down the hallway that opened to the foyer below, I saw our neighbor and his son nailing a piece of plywood over the front door from the inside. I went to Ron and told him it was time to make our peace with God.

Ron didn't hesitate. He agreed to pray with me. We said the Act of Contrition, and then we asked God's forgiveness for any wrongs we had done. We asked His blessings on our children, our families, and the people with us in the house. We asked Him to bless and protect the home that was our shelter in this storm, and we thanked Him for the many blessings He had given us. Then we said the Lord's Prayer. We didn't pray for long, but it was enough for me to come to the realization that I could face whatever was to come. I hoped it was enough for Ron, too. He seemed to be in shock and incapable of communicating with me.

I told Ron I wanted him to help me with a plan for getting out of the house if it became necessary. There was a window on the north end of the house with a small roof below it. We looked out that window and saw that two Sea-Doos, chained together, were stuck in a tree at the back of the house, one on either side of the tree. If we had to, I said, we could get to those Sea-Doos because they would float. I warned Ron that there was a possibility we would be trying to save our neighbor's grandson. He had a life jacket on, but he was so small that I wondered how we could safely carry him. We decided we would hold onto him through one of the armholes of the life jacket. I have no idea whether this would have been a good choice. I just felt the need to have a plan to help the child if necessary.

After that discussion, Ron and I joined our neighbor's wife in the upstairs hallway that opened to the foyer below. We were sitting, praying the rosary, when a huge wave burst through the front door.

The plywood that had been nailed over the door slammed into our neighbor; his son grabbed it and pulled it off of him. Then they both made their way up the stairs and joined us. We watched the bay come through the house and meet the river that was behind the house. Our place upstairs was well above the water, but we discussed moving into the attic if need be. There was a pull-down ladder, so the climb up would not be difficult, but I dreaded the thought of being up in that attic with the wind so strong and the water raging below us. My exit plan would not work under those conditions.

I went to the window I had planned to use as an exit and saw that the tree and the Sea-Doos were no longer there. My only plan now was to react, with the help of God, to whatever occurred. Mother Nature had complete control, and only God's will could prevail. If it was His will that we live, I thought, I would do everything I could to assist His efforts—I would be alert, quick thinking, and capable of making good decisions. Katrina would not deter me. Regardless of her mighty winds and powerful waves, I would be diligent, and I would fight back.

We gathered in the upstairs hallway overlooking the foyer, praying silently. I couldn't look at Ron; I couldn't look at anyone. I just watched the dark, threatening water whirling below us and prayed that God would protect this home, our only shelter, and allow us to prevail against this evil storm until she found her way past us and focused her destructive will in other directions. I considered this storm a living thing, an aberration—an angry, willful freak of nature filled with hate and venom. We were in the clutches of an unnatural energy intent on swallowing anything in its path. I feared this energy, but I also believed in my deepest being that with God's help, our collective will could and would outlast Katrina's.

Chapter 4 Katrina Leaves

Someone said in a very calm voice, "I think it's going down. The water's going down." And it was.

We watched as the watermark in the house became lower and lower. The winds were still strong, but their ferocity had eased, and at first I thought we might be in the eye of the storm. Actually, the storm had moved on shore just to the west of us, at Waveland. We spent the whole of the storm in the east quadrant, just outside the eye wall. The strongest part of Katrina had crossed Lopez Point, and we had survived her fury.

The water receded into the bay and back into the river very quickly. I was amazed that what had taken so many hours to occur ended with such speed. Once the water left the house, I borrowed a pair of rain boots and waded alone to the slab that once was the den, foyer, and dining room of our home. Part of the exterior wall, about three bricks high, was still standing, and I sat on that spot and wailed. I cried out all the stress and tension that had built up and been contained in me for days. No one could hear me because the wind was still so strong and loud.

All that was left was the slab ... and the memories of what had been.

Then I remembered my aunt when Ron and I found her the morning after Camille. She was so tiny and old. She was bruised from head to toe, and she was homeless. Yet when she saw me, she didn't cry—she smiled and told me she loved me, and she thanked us for coming to her so quickly. I determined right then that I would pull myself together. I would be strong, as all of us on the Mississippi coast are, and I would not upset my loved ones with my own worries. Now I recognize that this is the nature of my personality; I compartmentalize whatever I believe will hurt me or those who love me.

My decision to appear strong and brave was a good one, because very soon I would face people who cared about and loved us. People whose hearts broke for us would soon hold me in their arms and wish they could make life better again.

The first people I saw were neighbors who had been through the same hell we had experienced. We didn't have to say anything; we just held each other for a long time. I'm not sure where Ron was, and we've never discussed the fact that we went different ways when we could get outside. I just know that he suddenly appeared next to me, holding my mother's mauve raincoat. She had worn it the year before she died, and I had saved it in an upstairs bedroom. Ron showed it to me and said that we could clean it and it would be fine. He had found it behind the house at the tip of the point, twisted in the branches of a downed tree.

Not quite sure what to do with the fact that I had no home, I went back to our neighbor's house and began to mop the mud from her kitchen. I used water standing in the street to rinse the mop and tried doggedly to make the kitchen tiles reappear. When my neighbor came in to talk with me, I told her how fortunate we were that the big oak in my front yard had fallen across my driveway. The tree had prevented our car and truck from hitting the front of her house when the tidal surge washed them from their place in our garage. Now both mangled vehicles were pressed into the oak like grotesque metal appendages.

I recall telling our neighbor that both vehicles were full of mud and so we couldn't sleep in them. I wondered aloud where we would sleep. She said we would sleep right there, in their home. I appreciated her kindness, but in my heart, I wanted to be as far away from Lopez Point as I could get. Although I had forced myself to watch, I couldn't bear seeing the waves wash the orange clay from under the foundation of my home. And it went on for hours. I can still see bright-orange waves pounding their last blows against our home's foundation as they finally retreated into the bay.

I thanked our neighbor and left her in the kitchen of her once-beautiful home, now covered with and reeking from filthy mud.

As I walked back to where the front porch of our house had been, I noticed someone's truck embedded in the porch wall of our safe house during Katrina. I was perplexed at the number of unfamiliar vehicles twisted in trees and tangled in roofs that now lay on the ground. Down the street I saw my twin nieces, who with their husband and boyfriend were making their way toward us, trying with difficulty to walk around and through the debris—although *debris* doesn't really describe what covered our street and the places where adjacent homes once stood. Broken furniture, appliances, roof sections, wire, metal, insulation, and every imaginable kind of tree were piled high.

How ironic, I thought: I went to find my aunt after Camille, and now my nieces had come to find me after Katrina. As they cried and we hugged and talked, one of the twins dug down into the filthy mud and pulled out some teaspoons and a few other pieces of my silverware. "Look, Aunt Linda," she said, "it's some of your silver."

I'm not sure what I said to her, but I thought, *I don't want that silver. I don't want anything that reminds me of my life before Katrina. It is gone forever.* I looked away from my niece, and my eyes focused on a large oak tree whose branches draped dramatically over our pier. That lovely tree was intact, with plastic wrap twisted in its branches. On closer inspection, I realized that it was the plastic used to wrap chicken at the port. *My God,* I thought. *That blew here from Gulfport, twenty miles away.* It had landed in our tree and twisted around the branches so many times that it was about a foot thick. Many months later, the plastic wrap would be gone; some kind neighbor must have removed it or had it removed. Still, the image is as clear in my memory now as it was at the moment I first saw it.

Ron and I gathered our bag of important papers, my purse, and rain jackets and began to follow our family away from Lopez Point. We navigated around kitchen appliances, climbed over blown-down roofs, and passed our neighbors' broken treasures that were strewn about the street and lawns and hanging in the trees. We climbed over tree branches and tires and tons of shattered glass. We climbed over and walked through garbage. So much was unrecognizable; seven of the fourteen homes on our cul-de-sac were either gone or completely gutted, their ragged curtains and vinyl fascia blowing in the still-gale-force winds.

By dark we were at my niece's home. The clothes we wore that day were the only clothes we had. It was the strangest feeling to know we had no underwear, no nightclothes, no shorts or slacks or shirts or T-shirts. We each had one pair of shoes that were soaked with heavy, foul-smelling mud. We had no toiletries. Ron had no razor, and I had no hairbrush or makeup. It was as if we were newborns—we had nothing. Thanks to my niece and her husband, we soon had fresh clothes, toothbrushes, and toothpaste, and we were preparing to sleep on clean sheets. I have never been as grateful for the bonds and love of family as I was that night. Ron and I held each other, even in the August heat. We didn't speak. We just slept.

Chapter 5 A Community Vanishes

Very early the next morning, we awoke to the soft sounds of people talking. No birds were singing, and I realized how devastated our coastal community must be. Ron had been right. For us to sustain serious damage, all of Biloxi would have to flood ... and it had. From my nieces I learned that the Popps Ferry Bridge, which our area uses to reach the coastal cities, were missing long spans, as were the I-110 Bridge and the Cowan Road Bridge. That meant we had to travel Interstate 10 for a long distance to reach the areas of Gulfport and Long Beach where our family members lived. The beachfront looked like the scarred victim of an atomic bomb—there was not a habitable building for twenty-seven miles of Highway 90. To the east of our home, The Biloxi Point, long inhabited by fishermen and old Biloxi families, was now flat land with few trees and no homes. All the casinos were destroyed. Many casinos—huge structures—had been torn from their moorings and deposited onto the north side of Highway 90. The schools in Mississippi's six coastal counties and the cities within those counties were decimated. There were no gas stations left standing on Highway 90, and the inland stations soon ran out of gas.

Families who had gone to shelters had to remain there, as their homes were ruined. Hospitals became MASH units. The Mississippi Gulf Coast was gone and replaced with debris, death, and broken hearts.

Talking about the aftermath of Katrina kindled worry and fear in the twins, who wanted to reach their siblings and father. So they left on the long journey to find their family. Ron and I, now alone, still couldn't talk about our experience. He wanted desperately to return to the property and see if any of our belongings could be salvaged. I wanted to walk away. I loved the coast, but I wanted to be far away from the water. This would be the beginning of our battle for our future together.

My nephew took us back to the property, where it appeared that everything—*everything*—was gone. I was amazed that every possession we had accumulated over forty years had simply vanished. As I walked in a state of shock at what I was not seeing, I found two concrete statues: one was Mother Mary, and the other was a pelican. We'd had both for many years. I stood them up and tried to brush them off.

I thought of how often, after fires, earthquakes, or other disasters, survivors will say that what they'd lost was "just stuff"—at least they still had their lives. Well, for me, it wasn't just stuff. That included furniture and art that had been entrusted to us from generations long gone. It included handmade items given to me by my sister who had died of breast cancer. Somewhere in the mud of the bay rested my rosary and my mother's family Bible with handwritten notations of each new birth, marriage, and death. Our children's baby books, their diplomas, the china promised to my son when he married, my mother's engagement and wedding rings, my brother's first primary school reader, photograph albums documenting all the important events and precious ordinary moments of forty years of marriage and raising children, my entire treasured library, and so many other artifacts that served as a testament to our lives and those before us—that "stuff" was now gone. It would never return, just as those who gave that stuff to us for safekeeping would not return. Parts of our roots, our culture, and ourselves were gone and could never be brought back.

Although I had these thoughts, they were more like distant considerations. The reality of being homeless had only just begun to surface, with a very strong need to be acknowledged and addressed.

We returned to my niece's home and began to prepare the vienna sausage and crackers which would be our breakfast and lunch. The twins returned to report that my other niece and nephews and their father were all well. There was property damage, they said, but all of it could be repaired. I was so grateful for that news and to learn my brothers and sister and their families were safe. I had suspected that one of my brothers and my sister had lost their homes, and I was right. I also discovered that my grandparents' home, which my younger brother owned, had been twisted on its foundation. He would later repair the home and keep it in the family.

Sometime around mid-afternoon there was a knock on the door, and there stood our son. Michael had left Prattville at sunrise; trees were blocking his usual route, and the detours he had to take depended on his instincts. I held him for what must have felt like an eternity to him. After he and Ron took a drive to see our debris filled lot, they returned for me. We said our good-byes to our nieces and left for Prattville. My hope was that this would be the beginning of our starting over. I should have known that nothing I thought or planned would become reality for a very long while, if ever.

As night fell, the lack of streetlights and the terrible condition of the back roads we often had to use caused us to move slowly and cautiously. At some point we realized that we did not have enough gas to get through Mobile, Alabama, on our journey north to Prattville. When we came to a rest area, we decided to stop for the night and continue in the morning, driving for as long as our gas would last.

As we rested in the dark, trying to think clearly and devise a plan, a woman pulled off near us, her car filled with children and baggage. Then a truck packed with a family and its belongings pulled off, too. Michael and Ron approached the woman to ask if she had any gas we could buy. She answered with a resounding no. They then approached the man in the truck, whose response was very different. He gave us a couple of gallons of gas and would take no money for it.

We were again on our way, hoping to find an open gas station somewhere north of Mobile. We found one at a Walmart, with a departing line of some twenty vehicles. The attendant had just turned off the lights, signaling they were closed or out of gas. Michael and

Ron went to talk with the gas station clerk, and undoubtedly shared our plight; he filled our tank and would accept no money for the gas. We then pulled onto I-65 and, to our surprise, found an open Cracker Barrel restaurant. I knew how heaven tasted when I sipped that first cup of coffee!

It was late when we arrived in Prattville, but the Walmart was open. We went there and purchased the clothes and other items that would sustain us for a few days. Arriving at our son's home gave us a sense of connection akin to actually belonging somewhere. I cannot imagine how our son felt, knowing that his parents were homeless. All three of us seemed to be performing the same role. I would not cry or let down my pretense of control for fear of upsetting Michael. He would not allow his hurt to surface, so as not to upset us. Ron was already preparing to contact the insurance company and get the ball rolling so he could return and rebuild. Despite the fear and pain that we all felt, we chose to isolate those emotions within ourselves.

After two days of cleaning up with wet wipes, that first hot shower was wonderful. I couldn't help but think of our friends and family still trapped in the sweltering heat of the Mississippi coast. Those thoughts would permeate my life for many weeks. I felt constant guilt about fresh food, air conditioning, clean sheets and towels, telephone access, television, and just about every routine activity. The nagging thought of loved ones suffering through the aftermath of the storm—rationing their water and food, living without air conditioning or electricity, and facing the wreckage and devastation of our community—was ever-present and made even the simplest pleasure bittersweet.

It became apparent that my fingernails and toenails would not come clean. No matter how often or hard I brushed them, a muddy residue remained deep near the quick of my nails. There was a nail salon about three blocks from our son's subdivision, so I went there and explained what I thought I had under my nails: mud that I had mopped from my neighbor's kitchen floor. The ladies who ran the salon were angels. They brought me to a quiet little room where they lit candles and played soft, soothing music mixed with nature sounds, and they insisted I rest there and have tea before we did a manicure and pedicure. In those fifteen minutes of solitude I cried and cried and cried. All I can remember thinking is how much I wished I could have my mother hold me. I just wanted to relax and rest my head on her chest and cry out all my fear and disappointment. Only my mother could understand what I held deep inside, and I wanted so much to be understood without having to explain or rationalize my feelings. I didn't feel like the adult that I was. I felt vulnerable and weak.

When we finished the manicure and pedicure, my nails were back to normal, and the ladies would not accept any money for their services. It seemed that whenever someone could help, they wanted to do so, with no other reward than knowing they had made my day a little better. Angels were all around me.

Chapter 6 Hurricane "Corps of Engineers" Hits New Orleans

During our first days in Prattville, when we were still giving thanks that New Orleans had been spared a direct hit by Katrina, the levies protecting the city failed. We watched on television as the city we loved so much filled with muddy water. We watched families trapped on roofs, holding signs begging for help. We watched the Superdome, where we celebrated the Saints every year, become a prison for helpless, innocent people who had no water, food, or bathroom facilities, and very little hope. We did not then, nor do we now, understand how a major American city with a port that is critical to our country could be so devastated and yet so ignored. Babies died. Old people died. And still they were ignored. At the convention center, where Mardi Gras balls had thrilled us all, people died, their bodies placed outside and covered with whatever other people could find. Like human trash.

The shock of our experiences became even more overwhelming as we witnessed the unfolding tragedy of New Orleans. How can broken hearts continue to break? Ours did, every day.

Much later, after we had gotten through most of our major trials and when New Orleans could handle visitors, we returned to the Chateau. Our friends there expressed their love and their appreciation that we had not forgotten them and wanted to hear their stories. I will share one that was typical of the experiences of so many who faced the levies that had been built as protection for New Orleans by the Army Corp of Engineers.

Just as we did, New Orleanians prepared for the storm. Those who could afford to leave did. Those who couldn't either stayed home or went to shelters. This is the story of a family who stayed, thinking they would be fine.

After the storm, everyone in this family *was* fine—hot, missing electricity and city water, but fine. While the grandmother was washing a few dishes at the kitchen sink, using water the family had stored for this purpose, she heard an unfamiliar sound. As the sound became louder, she looked out the kitchen window and down the street. What she saw didn't register at first. When it did, she could only scream. Her husband heard her wails coming from the kitchen and ran to his wife. They literally trembled as they faced the realization that the levy some six blocks away had failed. They ran to their granddaughter and daughter who were outside, gathered them, and ran to the second floor of their home. Although they had grabbed purses and cell phones and a jug of water, these few items proved to be insufficient to help them. The house structure held, but as it filled with water they were forced into their attic. The attic had a small dormer that allowed them to climb onto the roof. There they stayed for several days, until a coast guard helicopter saw them, pulled them one at a time into the safety of the helicopter, and transported them to an area near an interstate ramp where other homeless, devastated New Orleanians were gathered.

There was no food or water, and the concrete overpass served as their protection from the sun. Hundreds of people were gathered there, and for days, no help came. Finally, buses arrived to take them out of the city, but there was no guarantee where their destination would be. The grandparents and the grandchild boarded one bus; there was no room for the daughter, the young child's mother. So she waited another day for the next bus. The first bus took the grandparents and grandchild to Houston; the second bus took the daughter to Atlanta. In these cities they were given cots, fresh clothes, food, water, toiletries, and shelter in churches and public facilities. Neither the daughter nor her parents had any idea where the other was taken. It took a year for them finally to unite.

This family had lived in their New Orleans home for four generations. The grandfather had worked in the hotel service industry for nearly forty years. As he told us his story, his eyes filled with tears as he said they had decided to settle in Houston. He had found work there, and so had his daughter. She was attending college in New Orleans when the levies broke, but she could not afford to resume her education. Their family home had been destroyed, and four generations of "stuff" had been destroyed with it.

The grandfather and I ended our visit sitting in the lovely courtyard of the Chateau, surrounded by tiny white lights that decorated the huge plants and vines that clung to the hotel walls. We faced each other, held hands over our knees, and cried. I don't know what has become of this family. I know there will never be truer New Orleanians than they were—their roots ran deep, as did their traditions and love for their city.

This is not an unusual story. Most stories, especially those from the city's Ninth Ward, are much worse. Generations died in the homes they cherished and worked so hard to maintain and keep in their families. These people, like the family whose story I shared, were not unhappy that they had had to work hard and had faced discrimination through the generations. That history was accepted and behind them. They were New Orleans. Their traditions—the Mardi Gras Indians and the Krewe of Zulu, their faith, their music and marching bands, their wonderful cooking and storytelling—built the foundation of New Orleans culture. They are so much of the heart of the city. And so much of the heart of the city has not been able to reestablish their homes, jobs, churches, traditions, and lives. Even today, I pray for them.

Chapter 7 Our True Trials Begin

Our first stay in Prattville lasted only about two weeks, as our daughter pled for us to come to her home in Centreville, Virginia. We were using a rental car for a few months until we could settle our minds, and so we drove to Virginia and stayed with Mary Margaret and Scott. From our first day in Prattville and throughout our first two weeks in Virginia, Ron called our insurance company and FEMA—*every day*. One day of busy signals, automated responses, and unanswered calls ran into the next.

Finally, at wit's end, Ron went to FEMA headquarters with a CNN reporter and cameraman. Eventually they were removed by security, but Ron did manage to complete the paperwork and get us into the system for a FEMA trailer on the Mississippi coast. He also reached our insurance company, only to be told that we were limited to making a flood claim; no one could collect for both flood and wind damage.

After a couple of weeks we returned to Prattville, hoping to get an appointment with our insurance company. In Prattville we would be close enough to home to make the appointment whenever the opportunity occurred. After a few days, the insurance company agreed to meet with us. We raced home, knowing they would reverse their decision when we told them what we and others had witnessed. If we could explain that the initial wind damage to our home was followed by damage from the raging waters, we could receive the insurance money we had bought and paid for over twenty years.

During the four-hour drive we were filled with hope. We would have an opportunity to explain, begin the process of recouping about a third of the value of our home, and plan how to start our lives over. Our hopes were unfounded. After all our telephone conversations with the insurance company, when we arrived they did not know who we were. We met with a temporary worker, a young man from another state who had been trained to repeat the mantra, "The flood took your house. We cannot pay your wind insurance." Within ten minutes I was so frustrated that I left to wait in the car. When Ron returned to the car thirty minutes later, his mood ranged from devastated to furious. We drove straight back to Prattville without even visiting family or friends. We knew that if they heard of our experience, it would only make them more upset.

The very next morning, Ron woke me saying he didn't know where his left arm was. He could move it, but he didn't know where it was. I took him to a nearby hospital, where we were told he had slept on his arm and restricted the circulation. Although he regained sensation while we were there, I would not let Ron accept this diagnosis. I asked for a referral to a neurologist, who saw us that afternoon. He ordered tests and determined that Ron had had a minor stroke, a "stroke event." He prescribed medication and sent us home to Prattville. I asked if that lightning strike a month or so before could have caused this. The doctor said he wasn't sure—there was some correlation between lightning strikes and strokes, but causation had not been proven. We were in shock and trying hard to keep life simple and calm.

When I told Mary Margaret what had happened and that it was serious, she flew to Birmingham with her little dog, Bitsy Belle. Michael met her at the airport and drove her to his home in Prattville. We were all together again and very confused and scared about what was happening in our lives. Still, I continued to pretend all was well. Mary Margaret had little patience with my attitude and challenged me to face the reality of our losses, but I was determined to keep that compartment closed.

A few days passed, and we found ourselves laughing at Bitsy Belle's antics. Michael had a big backyard with a privacy fence; his next-door neighbor had a huge lab. Bitsy Belle would bark and run to the wooden fence, trying to peer between the boards, and the lab's deep-throated bark would send her into a frenzy of running in circles. Then she would repeat the game she had created. What a joy she was, and is.

We were thrilled to return our rental car and purchase a new one like the one we had lost in Katrina. Ron, ever the loyal patron, decided he would buy a new truck, but only from our dealership on the coast—if and when it reopened. We went shopping and to dinner, and I talked about how life would return to normal and we would all be fine. Then, out of the blue, our insurance agent called and scheduled a meeting on the slab of our home for 9:00 a.m. the following Saturday. We were so excited.

Meanwhile I had been in communication with a colleague at the university who was teaching my course so as to minimize disruption for my graduate students. When I called to tell her I would come meet my class the following Saturday, she insisted I stay with her and her husband in their guest bungalow. Then she invited us to live there, free, while Ron rebuilt or bought a home.

Ron and I discussed the plan for the upcoming Saturday. Mary Margaret would delay her return to Virginia and go with us to the coast; Michael would drive. Then Ron and Michael would stay with my nieces, and Mary Margaret and I would stay at my friend's bungalow. Ron knew he would have to take his medicine and stay hydrated, but his doctor thought the trip would be fine. Life was beginning to make some sense.

We left for the coast very early Friday morning. As we passed through Mobile we were stopped by congested traffic, and Ron did the strangest thing: he saw a partially filled water bottle alongside the highway, and he jumped out of the car, saying we might need that water. He retrieved the bottle but would not return to the car. Michael pulled off the highway and into a gas station while Ron was in the midst of traffic, acting erratically. We finally got him back into the car and settled. His behavior was a forewarning of a devastating stroke, but we didn't recognize it at the time.

When we arrived on the coast, I dropped Ron and Michael at the dealership where Ron would purchase his new truck. We would meet at the home of my younger brother, who was now living with his family in a camper in their backyard. Mary Margaret and I went to the property for her to see it for the first time since it was destroyed by Katrina. While this needed to happen for her, she was crushed. She cried and sobbed uncontrollably and dug in the mud and trash, looking for the life she knew was gone. After a time, we walked down the pier and used bay water to wash the mud from her hands, knees, and feet. I held her as she wept. It broke my heart to feel the pain she was in, just as it broke her heart to realize what we must have experienced. Our emotions were raw by the time we reached my brother's home. We had driven there in silence. Seeing the total destruction, mile after mile, was overwhelming, a reality that could not be altered by anything we could say.

When Ron got out of his new truck at my brother's home, his smile was worth the world to me. Because he was laughing and upbeat, everyone's mood improved. He had his truck back. I had my car. He was going to solve the insurance situation the next morning, and I was going to teach my graduate students and work out the plans for our stay in the bungalow. For the first time in several weeks, we didn't feel like homeless gypsies, and we had a plan. Yet when I kissed Ron good-bye and Mary Margaret and I pulled away, I felt a deep sadness. He looked suddenly old and tired, and unusually anxious, but hiding it. I just didn't want to leave him. But our plans were made, so I did. It is a decision I regretted then and still regret today.

*Our nephew and Ron excited because this was the morning Ron
would meet with the insurance agent on our slab. The agent
never came. Ron's stroke was just a few hours away.*

Mary Margaret and I had dinner at the home of my colleague
and her husband. We talked about my course and how surprised my
students would be to see me the next morning, and we talked about
a book we planned to write together while Ron and I lived in the
bungalow. We discussed everything except the storm. In spite of good
food, good company, and lovely accommodations, I had a difficult time
sleeping that night. Early in the morning, I left our daughter sleeping
and had coffee with my friend on her back porch. Then I left for the
university.

My class was overwhelmed and delightfully surprised to see me. There
were hugs all around, and for a couple of hours we just talked about what
we had experienced. Katrina had torn up their hometowns, too. They
had gone without water and electricity. They had either eaten at a church
or worked at a church, feeding others. Their schools were damaged and
still had not reopened.

Eventually, our class became a class again, and I felt wonderful
teaching—like I could finally exhale. I was calmer than I had felt in
weeks.

When I walked from the building after class, I saw my colleague pull into the parking lot with our daughter. I smiled and yelled, "It was a wonderful day. Why are ya'll here?" The look on my friend's face told me something was very wrong, as did our daughter running toward me with her dog and our suitcase. "I don't want to tell you this, but Daddy is in the emergency room at Biloxi Regional," she said. "They think he had another stroke."

I drove home at more than ninety miles an hour, sitting on my horn, my car's emergency lights blinking, with Mary Margaret hanging out the car window, motioning for other cars to move over. We were stopped momentarily by a highway patrolman, who listened to our situation and let us go with the warning that we could be killed if I continued to drive as I had been. I continued to drive as I had been while talking with an emergency room doctor who wanted permission to give my husband an injection of anti-clotting medication that could either save his life or cause irreparable damage, and possibly death. I could hardly think straight, but when our son said that the doctor would not accept his signature for permission, I agreed to the shot.

When we arrived at the hospital, the shot had not been administered—they were waiting for me to sign the permission papers. Ron was gray, his face distorted. He could only make gurgling sounds, and he couldn't feel or move the left side of his body. He was hooked to all sorts of equipment, none of which could do more than keep him alive until I signed the papers, which I did. Then we sat by his side and prayed for God to let us keep him. I prayed for another chance to hold him and let him know how much I loved him, another chance to tell him what a wonderful husband and father he had been and how happy my life was because of him. I wanted him to know I didn't care that we hadn't evacuated or that we had lost our home. I didn't care about anything but him staying with me.

Ron was critical but alive, and the Biloxi hospital could not care for him. I was given two choices: we could move him to a Navy ship's offshore hospital, which had been made available because Katrina had devastated the local hospitals, or we could move him to a hospital neurology unit in Pascagoula; the unit was overcrowded but willing to take him. I chose Pascagoula.

We went there by ambulance that night, the kids driving behind us in Ron's new truck and my car. The days and nights that followed are a blur. Highlights I can remember, but even those seem foggy, unwilling to become clear.

Chapter 8 One Day at a Time

At first we could not be with Ron; we had to stay in a waiting area outside the neurological intensive care, where the doctor and nurses did whatever they did to sustain him. We waited there all night.

The next morning they allowed us to see Ron. He was still paralyzed and had a tube in his mouth to collect saliva and prevent him from choking. He could not swallow, and even with my ear to his lips I couldn't really understand what he was trying to tell me. We were allowed to stay for only about five minutes a few times a day.

We ate at the hospital, and after several days we were allowed to shower in a public restroom that had once been a bathroom for emergency room doctors. The locks on the doors had been removed, so whenever possible, one of us would shower while another of us stood outside the door. On occasion we would shower, dry, and dress inside the tiny stall and then step out to find someone using the toilet or washing his hands. There was no personal space, no privacy, and we were surrounded by strangers who were as broken as war refugees. We slept in the car and in the back of the truck. We washed our underwear in the bathroom sink and hung it to dry on the bumper of the car.

One morning a hospital administrator told me we could sleep on the floor of the radiology waiting room, very near Ron, as long as we left when the cleaning crew arrived at 4:30 or 5:00 a.m. I remember how grateful I was. I claimed a spot under the receptionist's desk, for fear of being stepped on in the dark. The kids slept on the "living room" floor—a space between two parallel rows of waiting room chairs with a television at one end and an open area at the other. Bitsy Belle couldn't stay with us, so Mary Margaret left her with a cousin, visiting with her little dog when she went there to wash the clothes she and Michael had purchased at a dollar store near the hospital. We had driven home from Prattville with a single change of clothing, thinking we would return in twenty-four hours; we ended up staying for weeks. Still, being able to sleep inside the hospital was so much better than sleeping in the car or truck. Even with the car windows down, the heat was oppressive; it was no place for our children or even Bitsy Belle. I never left the hospital. Friends and family came to us, although travel was very difficult. Part of the I-10 Bridge into Pascagoula had been destroyed, and only one lane was open. Yet they came and they prayed for us, and they kept us in their hearts. Our priests visited and prayed for us. The director of gifted education in our state department of education contacted the directors from other states. They spread the word about our need for prayers, and groups from across the whole country prayed for Ron and our family.

Early one morning in October, I was drinking coffee in the hospital cafeteria when a nurse came and asked if she could sit with me. I agreed, happy to have the company. She asked what had happened to us, so I shared most of our story. She then put her hand on mine, bowed her head, and was silent for a while. When she looked up at me, she said she knew we would all be fine. She told me I was a strong woman and that I had so much love to give that she knew God would spare Ron and allow me to give him my strength and love. I thanked her for listening and sharing her faith. One day, I said, I would write our story, and she would be one of the angels I wrote about. She smiled and left. I never saw her again.

When I returned to see Ron, the doctor told me he was being moved to a room near intensive care, where we could be with him. I still get a chill thinking about that morning; I felt so strong, so ready to love Ron back to health. I was ready for anything that day. We thought Ron looked great! He was showing expression again, and he was so improved that I let Michael take a picture of him. Ron was going to come back to us—we could see it on his face.

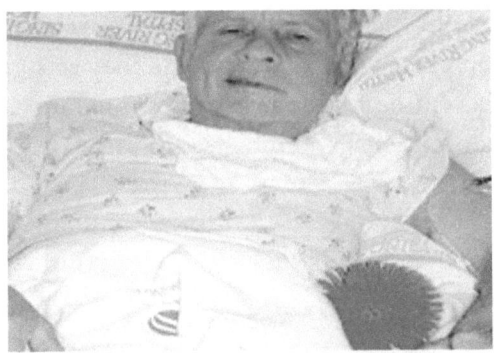

Ron in his own room; finally we could be with him.

Now that Ron had a chance at life, I can reflect on what actually occurred on the Saturday morning when he had his terrible stroke. Ron and Michael were at our property at the agreed-on time of nine o'clock.

The street view of our property after Katrina, with the sign identifying the address and insurance company.

Neighbors had not begun to repair their homes, but the street was clear. Still, the oak lay across our driveway, our vehicles had not been moved yet, there were piles of debris everywhere, and the foundation of our home teetered, the fill clay washed from beneath it. Neighbors had placed on our slab items they recognized as ours— little things like a coffee cup or a vase or framed picture. The picture would be ruined, but they thought we might want the frame.

Neighbors left on our slab items of ours they had found.

It was very hot, and Michael insisted that Ron remain in the air-conditioned truck until the insurance agent arrived. After an hour or so of waiting, Ron left the cool truck. He walked among the destruction in the oppressive heat, becoming more and more upset. Michael knew it would only upset his father further if he protested too much, so he walked with him, ensuring that he drank enough water and encouraging him to go to the truck periodically to get cool. The insurance agent never arrived.

*Ron waiting for our insurance agent and seeing his truck and my car,
which had washed into the oak that fell across the driveway.*

As noon approached, our son convinced his dad to leave, and they started to the truck. Ron looked at our son and tried to speak, but he was gurgling on a foamy liquid that suddenly began to spill from his mouth. Michael carried him to the truck and drove him to the nearby country club, where they called for emergency medical help. As Ron was transported to the hospital, Michael called his sister, setting in motion our return to Biloxi.

I often think about how strong our children are. The trauma of it all, everything they went through, makes it clear how resilient, how well-grounded human beings can be.

Only four years earlier, our son-in-law, Scott, had been scheduled to fly from Boston to Los Angeles. The evening before his morning flight, he was told to fly a different route to substitute for an ill pilot. He flew from Boston to San Diego that night, but he saw no reason to wake Mary Margaret to tell her of the change. The next morning, the flight from Boston to Los Angeles was hijacked and flown into the World Trade Center. For an entire day—until Scott could finally get through to Mary Margaret and tell her he was safe in San Diego—we all thought he was the pilot or copilot on that hijacked plane.

A few months later, Michael was in the first deployment to Iraq. He was responsible for establishing the Baghdad airport as a base for our troops to use as they entered the country. Because of his job, he had a telephone that could be used for emergencies only. We knew not to call our son unless it was a true emergency.

Since the scare of September 11, Mary Margaret would have nightmares, awakening to loud sounds that didn't exist. She was confronted daily with the reality of terrorism, since she and Scott lived in Fairfax County, just minutes from Dulles International Airport and very near Washington, DC. At school, she watched other teachers hoarding water and taping their classroom windows. One evening she awoke with a terrible feeling about her brother, so she went downstairs and called him on that emergency phone. She explained that she had had a bad feeling and wanted to know he was okay.

Michael assured his sister he was fine and they hung up, although she still felt uneasy. Later, Michael admitted that when she called, he and other soldiers were under fire at the airport; they were behind bunkers while the perimeter just outside the airport was being defended. When his tour of duty was finished, he was stationed at Dover Air Force Base, Delaware, where he handled the return of soldiers killed in action.

Both our children had seen such a harsh side of life, and now Katrina was reinforcing that harshness, reshaping our lives in ways we could not imagine.

Our children seldom left my side while Ron was in the Pascagoula hospital. Our daughter took Family Medical Leave, and our son used all his leave time. They never questioned their decision to stay, and I can never repay their love and support. Parents don't expect to become the responsibility of their children at the ages Ron and I were. But Ron was fighting for his life, and I suddenly had such a burden of responsibility that without our children there, I don't know what would have happened.

When Ron was moved to a room where we could stay with him, I was awarded the foldout chair as my bed. I moved from my spot under the desk in the radiology waiting room to Ron's room. I cannot express how much better I felt being with him all the time. His mouth had to be suctioned and he was on a feeding tube, so I learned how to use both. Staph infections had become an issue in the hospital, and clean as we might, the site where Ron's feeding tube was inserted became infected. It had to be cleaned and bandaged daily, and his urine output monitored—tasks I handled without reservation.

I was determined that Ron would talk to me. As the days and nights passed and the physical therapists worked tirelessly with him, his speech returned, his facial expressions became more normal, and he learned to sit up in bed with assistance. The first time the therapists stood him up on his feet, I thought I would be the next one in intensive care—I was so protective, so afraid that he would be hurt. The therapists were wonderful, talented, confident young people. They gave us such hope. Eventually we began to wean Ron off the feeding tube, and he began to swallow. What progress that was! I was so sad to learn that one of Ron's favorite therapists, a high school classmate of Mary Margaret's, committed suicide a few years after Katrina. Since we knew him, we trusted him, and he was an important factor in Ron's recovery. He was a fine young man and such a talented therapist. His death is a loss for so many others he could have helped. How sad that no one could help him.

Our son had been in contact with the car dealership where Ron had bought his truck the day before his stroke, and they agreed to take the truck back and refund our money. The kids went to take care of this. What good people at that dealership! They sent their best wishes to Ron and me and said they would pray for his recovery. Meanwhile, our son contacted a close college friend, an emergency medical technician living in northern Alabama; he contacted other friends and obtained an air-conditioned trailer that he brought to us in Pascagoula. His precious wife had packed the trailer with goodies. The hospital let us hook it up in an unused area of the parking lot that had an electric hookup. Now the kids had a place to sleep. We ate homemade brownies and drank milk and were amazed at our good fortune.

Our son helped me collect on our flood insurance and took me to a temporary branch of our mortgage company, where I paid off the house. I was relieved not to have the worry of making mortgage payments on a trash-filled lot, but sad to realize how little we had owed on a home that was now destroyed.

I was gone less than an hour and returned to see Mary Margaret sleeping in a chair beside her father. She and Michael went for coffee, and while Ron was still resting, our insurance agent called to check on him. It was now several weeks past the Saturday when we were supposed to have met with this agent. This was our first conversation, and it was not a pleasant one. He argued that it was unreasonable for us to expect our homeowner's insurance to pay for wind damage when we had already received payment for flood damage. After more than fifteen years of having a friendly, trusting professional relationship with our insurance company, it was difficult to come to the realization that I would have to hire an attorney to handle our claim, as so many people of the Mississippi coast had to do. But I knew when we hung up that I would have no other choice.

I was very worried about Ron's staph infection. It didn't appear to be healing, and the doctor would not remove the feeding tube as long as the site was infected. The doctors were more concerned with moving him to the therapy floor. One of my twin nieces, a hospital social worker with whom I had been in frequent communication, said she was worried about Ron being placed on the therapy floor too soon. But I trusted the doctor.

So Ron was relocated to the therapy floor, and I would no longer be allowed to stay in his room with him. It took me about thirty minutes to gather my few possessions and move them to the trailer, where I would share a spot with our daughter. I chose to move while Ron was being evaluated in the physical therapy "gym." He couldn't sit without being tied in the chair; he couldn't stand or even adjust his body without help. He could hold his head erect and look to his right. He had what was termed "left-side neglect," meaning he was not aware of anything to his left. Consequently, he never looked there.

When I got off the elevator to take Ron's things to his new room, I was shocked. He was slumped in a wheelchair in the area near the elevator, mouth agape, staring to the right and down at the floor. Next to him was an older woman in a wheelchair, crying. I saw stars! I took Ron to his room and enlisted assistance to get him settled. Then I called my niece and told her she was right—he wasn't ready for the therapy center.

My niece explained that if he stayed there for twenty-four hours, he would have to stay there for several months, and he would not be allowed to change to a different therapy location without loss of insurance coverage. This was a rule that insurance companies and Medicare had made. With the unrelenting staph infection and Ron's obvious lack of capacity for therapy, I knew I could not allow him to stay there for months. I went to the hospital social worker and told her I wanted to move Ron to Spain Rehabilitation Center at the University of Alabama at Birmingham. I had heard wonderful things about UAB and had already planned to take him there when he was well enough. Now there was not time to wait.

My communication with the social worker was not a good experience until my niece intervened. Then the wheels began to turn. At UAB, however, we hit a brick wall: the doctor would not accept Ron because of the feeding tube and the staph infection. I called her, explaining what we had been through, how very sick Ron was, and how terribly he needed the care UAB could give him. She called me back and said they would take him.

Our son's EMT friend arranged for his company to come to Pascagoula and take Ron by ambulance to Birmingham. This wonderful friend drove the transfer and refused payment for his work. When it was time, this same young man returned the trailer to Mobile. What an angel he was. We never could have had smooth pathways without him.

Ron was moved back to his original room and scheduled to leave the next morning. Late that night I was sitting alone, drinking coffee in the cafeteria. I was feeling kind of dizzy and wondering what was wrong with me when a man asked if he could sit with me. I thought that might be a good idea, since we were the only two in the area; if I was sick, I might need someone to go for help. But I soon forgot to worry about my dizziness. He needed someone to listen, and listen I did.

He and his wife had been in Katrina, too, washed from their home on the Biloxi Point. His wife sustained serious injuries to her legs from debris. She was also cut badly in many places, and bacteria in the water had entered her bloodstream. She had been in the hospital, taking powerful intravenous antibiotics, for weeks without improvement. Now she was at a critical point. The doctors had told them one of her legs would have to be amputated the next morning, and there was a strong possibility that the other leg would also have to be removed if the infection continued to rage. My heart broke for that poor man and his wife. They had been married thirty years and had raised three children. Their home was paid off, and now it was gone.

I just listened and never thought to share our story. His story was so powerful, his situation so tragic, that I forgot about ours. After some time, he thanked me for listening and asked me to pray that his wife would live, with or without her legs. "I can't bear to live without her," he said. When he left, I sat there alone and cried.

It was then that I began to ask why this had happened to our community. *We are a caring, loving community. We've always done our best to look after one another and follow the rules of good morals and ethics. Why are so many of us suffering?* I went up to Ron's room, where he slept pressed up against the right rail of the bed. He felt unprotected if he couldn't feel something next to him, and so he always managed to inch his way to the right rail. I stayed there in the chair next to his bed and talked softly about all the wonderful experiences we had had. At some point I fell asleep.

The next morning I was so dizzy I couldn't stand. I vomited and was sweating as though I had cut the grass in noonday heat. My daughter took me to the hospital's emergency room, where I was diagnosed with an inner-ear condition that required me to take a medication that would put me to sleep. This was our day to travel to Birmingham—a terrible time for me to become ill.

When we returned to Ron's room, I was in a wheelchair, unable to stand without falling over and vomiting. A new nurse had come on duty and, in my absence, had helped Ron to the toilet and left him there. She obviously did not understand the gravity of his condition. When she returned to help him back to bed, she found him on the floor between the toilet and the wall. She was a big woman and didn't think she would need assistance to get him up. In doing so she lifted him from his paralyzed side, pulling his left shoulder out of joint. The doctor was there when we arrived; he had done what he could to correct the problem and was taping Ron's arm and shoulder to keep them in place. Now the same nurse had to clean his feeding tube site because I wasn't capable of doing it. Ron refused to have her do it, and we left with some of the nurses crying their good-byes and the poor nurse who had hurt Ron crying alone in his room. It was a terrible way to have to leave. I had grown to love the staff and had no flowers or fruit basket or anything to express my appreciation for all they had taught me and the care they had shown Ron and our family.

Mary Margaret drove me to Birmingham, while Michael rode ahead in the ambulance with his father. I know our daughter stayed right behind them all the way to Birmingham, but I couldn't watch the ambulance because whenever I opened my eyes, a wave of nausea overcame me. I slept the whole way. When we arrived, I was weak but able to function. I didn't realize how much better life was about to become.

Chapter 9 A Chance to Heal

Our new home would be a large hospital room with an unusually large bathroom. Nurses told us that our room and the adjacent laundry room was the suite where Governor George Wallace recuperated from his attempted assassination many years ago. The two women who would be Ron's doctors arrived shortly after we settled. I could tell they were bright and intensely interested in Ron's condition. When they examined his feeding tube site, they immediately wrote orders for an antibiotic, a specific ointment, and a cleaning three times a day.

I explained how involved I had been with Ron's care and asked if that would continue at Spain. They agreed that I would be trained by the nurses and therapists, and they offered me a foldout couch in Ron's room or a small apartment near the hospital. I chose the couch and was given sheets, pillows, a blanket, towels, and toiletries. A nurse showed me the laundry room and where the detergent was, showed me where the linens and towels were kept, and took me to the area where I could find hot coffee most of the day. I was also shown where the bandages were and which ones Ron would need. Within twenty minutes I had met the nursing staff and knew where everything we would need was located.

When I returned to Ron, he was clean and shaved, had special inflatable covers on his legs, and was settled in his bed, being fed a late-afternoon pureed lunch that looked terrible to me. Ron loved it. He said it tasted like homemade chicken soup.

Our kids stayed for a little while and then headed back to Prattville in my car, Bitsy Belle in tow. She had come into Ron's room, secretly tucked away in our daughter's purse, after all the staff had gone. Ron was so happy to see her; Mary Margaret promised to bring her back soon. After they left, I crawled into the bed with Ron and just held him. I reassured him that now he would get better—I just knew it. We were finally in a place where we could both heal, and we could heal together. I woke up next to Ron when his dinner arrived.

His pureed supper tasted like split pea soup with ham. He was very happy to have it, and he also liked his "pudding"—Ensure that had been whipped until it was thick. He had two of these because they tasted so good. Ron had lost a lot of weight, and I knew he was on the mend because he looked so forward to meals.

Early the next morning, a nurse's assistant came in and wrote the day and date on a whiteboard below the clock on the wall across from Ron's bed. She brought him a warm, wet washcloth for his face and chatted with him a minute before she left and returned with his breakfast: pureed oatmeal with syrup and coffee and milk. She followed this routine every morning, and we knew this was going to be a good place. All the liquids they served Ron had a thickening powder dissolved in them. He never noticed.

A little while after that first breakfast, one of Ron's doctors came in with a very large male doctor. He examined Ron's feeding tube and, without warning, leaned over Ron and asked him to take a deep breath. Then the doctor literally popped the tube out—it made a loud pop, and then it was out. Later Ron's regular doctor told me she knew she wasn't strong enough to extract the tube and had enlisted the strongest doctor she could find to do the deed. With the tube gone, the frequent cleanings with new ointment, and the antibiotics, Ron's staph infection began to clear up and was practically gone within a week. Because I cleaned the site regularly, I could see the progress right before my eyes.

Our first trip to the therapy gym was a powerful experience that showed us how much would be expected of Ron. Ron stood behind a tall walker, his left hand secured by an ace bandage to the handle, while a therapist sat on a little rolling stool and moved Ron's foot in a walking motion. Ron was walking! For this activity, I would usually roll the wheelchair. Then he was placed on a mat where he helped move his own leg as it was exercised by a therapist. I learned how to help Ron do this and most of his other exercises as he went from one therapy station to the next.

In the middle of morning therapy, his nurse arrived and gave him his meds, always with applesauce. Ron worked hard all morning, went to his room for lunch, returned to the gym, and worked all afternoon. At lunch he had to sit up in his wheelchair, supported by wedges to keep him upright. Even mealtime was part of the therapy. Before he could eat, he had to trace the edge of the tray all the way around and identify each item on the tray. He also had daily speech therapy, during which electrodes were attached to his neck and shocked his throat muscles. He ate colored applesauce that was observed on a screen as it went down his throat.

Ron and Linda learning the power of electricity during rehab at Spain Rehab Center at UAB, 2005. Ron's left hand is paralyzed but was exercised electronically.

On Veteran's Day Ron was honored with a special tag, which he wore all day. His picture was put on a bulletin board along with pictures of the other veterans there, and the speech therapy staff sang patriotic songs and did a little dance routine to entertain them.

Within two weeks, Ron was a different person. He sat without help in his wheelchair and could use his special walker without the therapist moving his foot—he actually picked his foot up and put it down by himself. Then they started water therapy. Three days a week, Ron was in a pool, walking with his therapist and smiling the entire time. He actually laughed aloud for the first time in many months. Still, he was quite serious about his therapy, and he did his very best at every session.

Ron during pool therapy at Spain Rehabilitation Center, UAB.

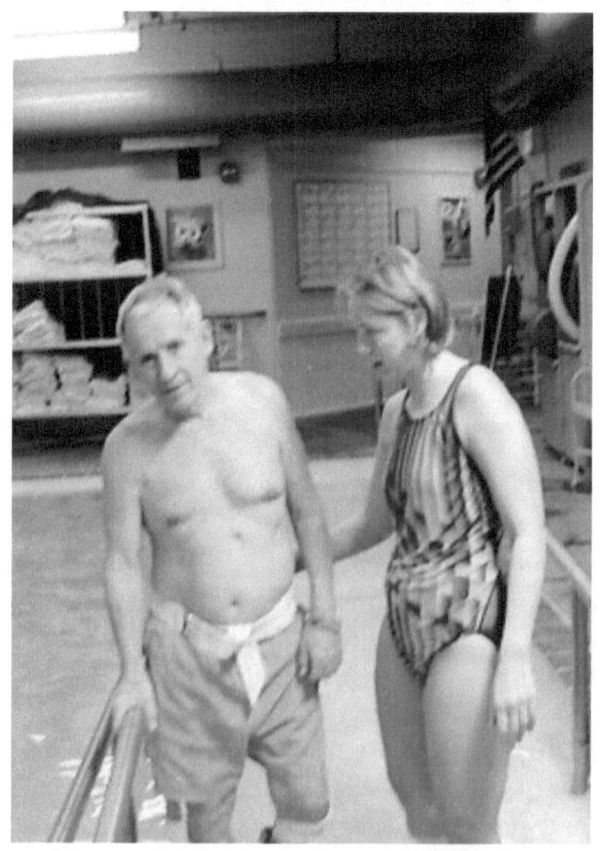

Ron walking out of the pool at Spain Rehabilitation Center, UAB.

Our kids could not believe his progress. He talked clearly, and his face looked normal. When Mary Margaret returned to Virginia, we were sad not to have her visits, but we were ready to handle life at Spain Rehab on our own. Michael visited on the weekends and always praised his dad's progress, which made us both proud.

One day while Ron was on the toilet, he complained of severe pain in his stomach and rectum. When I checked, the toilet was full of blood. In a panic, I pulled the chord for the nurse, who snapped into action. The doctor determined it was probably a rupture caused by diverticulitis; there was nothing they could do until the bleeding stopped and they could perform a colonoscopy. Ron bled for days and was not allowed out of bed. He had three blood transfusions. I was tortured thinking he could die from this problem. He had made such remarkable progress, and now this critical setback.

When the bleeding finally stopped, they did the colonoscopy and determined that it was a ruptured diverticula and Ron would be fine. I'm convinced that had we been anywhere else when that happened, Ron would have bled to death—those nurses and doctors saved his life. At one point there was blood all over me, the bed, the floor, and the nurse, but she handled the situation in a calm way that made me confident everything would be fine. And it was.

Not long afterward, as I slept one night, I heard Ron trying to wake me. I tried to awaken but just couldn't seem to get out of my foggy dream state. I could hear him and understand him, but I couldn't make my body move or my eyes open. This had never occurred to me before and has not reoccurred. Ron kept telling me to look by the bathroom door because Jesus was standing there. Then I could hear Ron speaking in a soft tone, as if he were agreeing with someone who was in the room with us. Still, I couldn't wake myself up.

The next morning I assumed I had dreamed the experience and didn't mention it to Ron. But when the doctor came in, Ron told him that he had seen Jesus just inside his room, by the bathroom door. My heart stopped. I moved closer to hear Ron describe how Jesus had looked, dressed all in white and very bright, as if the light had been turned on in the room. He said Jesus had told him that the people at this hospital were very special to Him, and that Ron should tell them all how much Jesus loved them for the way they helped people. I didn't speak; I'd been so sure I had just been dreaming. And I didn't know what to expect from the doctor. But he just took Ron's hand and thanked him for sharing his experience. "Faith is the most powerful healing force anyone could have," he said.

When the doctor left, I asked Ron to tell me what had happened during the night, and he explained that he had been awakened by Jesus calling his name. He said he had tried to wake me up, but Jesus told him His message was meant for Ron alone—that He loved Ron and all the people who worked in this hospital, and that Ron should tell all the caregivers that they and the hospital were blessed. Then Jesus was gone.

I accepted Ron's experience because it was so real to him, and he shared his story with all his nurses and therapists. Regardless of what occurred that night, I know this: the people at Spain Rehabilitation Center at the University of Alabama were very special, and so was their hospital. There was no negativity or question of whether or not Ron would recover to a functional level. Every day his caregivers inspired confidence in us. Ron's stay at Spain was filled with not only high quality care, but with a love for us and a belief in us that motivates us even today. For me, for us, they were angels.

Several friends and family members made the trip to Birmingham to see us. I was so proud to roll Ron to the outdoor courtyard and enjoy coffee, tea, and snacks with our visitors. Everyone now realized that Ron was out of jeopardy and would come home one day. Now that we had visitors coming to see us, I shopped for a few clothes that didn't come from Pascagoula's dollar store or Prattville's Walmart, and I found a beauty shop and had my hair done and got a manicure and pedicure. The hairdresser was precious, a beautiful woman with a quick smile, friendly personality, and very good skills. She offered to come to Spain and cut Ron's hair.

Ron was delighted. After she left, everyone on our floor was talking about the beautiful woman who had cut Ron's hair. And Ron had a story to tell, too. When his haircut was finished, the hairdresser told him she wanted him to remember her. As she walked away, she pulled the back of her pants down to a dangerously low point, revealing a tattoo that said "Loomis Cargo" in a fancy script. Now, she said, Ron would think of her whenever he saw a Loomis Security sign or armored truck! How we laughed at her antics, and how fondly we remember her today. When I went to her salon, it was one of just three times I left Ron in three months. I hated to go, and I worried the whole time. But he was fine when I returned, and my meeting that special person resulted in so many happy moments as Ron told his story. I am glad I was able to bring her into his life.

During each of our last few days at Spain, I took Ron to the cafeteria for a meal with me. It's a long way from Ron's room to the cafeteria; where we had to use a covered hallway that connected two parts to the hospital. It spanned four lanes of traffic below us. We did very well. I now knew I was capable of handling outings, therapy, cooking the right foods, maintaining the medication schedule, and Ron's showers and dressing. The people at Spain Rehab Center gave us our lives back.

Ron taking a treat back to his room at Spain Rehabilitation Center, UAB.

The day before we left Spain, Ron's therapists took us out to lunch at a nearby restaurant. We walked there. This was when I learned to handle public restrooms and move the wheelchair up and down curbs. It was a bittersweet time for Ron and me; I knew we were ready to spread our wings, but I also knew I would miss the wonderful people at Spain.

Ron and Linda having lunch with Ron's therapists.

When it was time for us to leave Spain, both doctors were there to hug us and assure me they were just a phone call away. Ron's therapists and nurses all stopped by, too, and shared hugs and kisses. These precious people had filled the cracks in our hearts with happy memories and love.

We entered the cab for the airport, and as we pulled away, the therapists and nurses stood and waved good-bye. I think they felt like proud parents, and to some extent I felt as though we were the children they had raised to be capable and independent in our new life.

Scott and Mary Margaret had found us a nice apartment in Fairfax, Virginia, about fifteen minutes from their home in Centreville. I looked so forward to finally having a place of our own. Mary Margaret had rented lovely furniture for our apartment, which she had decorated with touches of elegance and fun. Everything was done for us, from televisions in the living room and bedroom to a computer station. The pantry and laundry room were stocked. Our cable television and telephone service were all set. Fresh flowers on the dining table actually coordinated with the kitchen décor and the living room curtains. Our bedroom was ready with scented candles and personalized leather bags filled with new toiletries. Even the bathrooms had special towels, bubble bath and lotions, and scented candles. Our daughter and her husband had worked very hard to be certain that we would smile as soon as we arrived. They had even set a little bistro table on our front porch and hung a welcome wreath on our door. I am certain they waited for us at Dulles International Airport with great anticipation—but first we had to get there!

Chapter 10 The Atlanta Airport

Our flight from Birmingham to Atlanta was smooth and uneventful, and my confidence soared. Our travels from Atlanta to Dulles, however, were an absolute nightmare. There was not enough time for us to get from our arrival gate to our departure gate in the Atlanta airport. If you've ever been there, you'll understand why we needed the extra time. But that was something we did not have.

When I made the travel arrangements, I was assured that the arrival and departure gates were no more than ten to twelve minutes apart, even with a wheelchair. When we were met by the airline assistant who would get us from the arrival to the departure gate, she took a brief look at the tickets, shook her head, and barked into her phone. Then we were off at a slow run.

To my amazement, she took us through the bowels of the Atlanta airport, underground areas I didn't know existed. We went through baggage areas and storage rooms, through doors and up elevators as our trot turned into a breakneck pace. As if we weren't already panicked enough, when we arrived at the gate and were through the boarding gate, we discovered that the jet was not attached at the dock—it was out on the tarmac! Our guide barked into her phone again, and a tractor-type vehicle with a lift came to the dock. Ron was rolled onto a small platform. His chair was parked, wheels locked, in front of a very large man who apparently was in charge of Ron's transfer. I had to go downstairs and out onto the tarmac to the jet, where I waited in the jet door for Ron to be transported there like luggage. The platform transporting him had clear, heavy plastic around it to protect him (or the luggage for which I am certain this equipment was normally used) from the elements. I stood in the doorway, my heart in my throat, watching Ron come nearer and nearer; I knew he would be upset and afraid. Instead, I saw him smiling and laughing and talking with his "captor." I finally exhaled when he was rolled on board and to our seat. He was chattering about his adventure, and all I could think about was the glass of wine I would order when we were in flight!

Once we were settled, the flight was lovely, and after we landed and retrieved the wheelchair, we walked the connector hallway and saw Mary Margaret and Scott waiting for us. It was a wonderful reunion.

When we saw our new home we were delighted! Our daughter had cooked dinner, and we all sat at the table in our new home and enjoyed our visit while we ate. After the dishes were done and the kids had left, we settled into bed in our nightclothes and flipped on the evening news. We were home, we were alone, and we were ready to see how successful we could be starting this new life together.

A few days after we arrived, our son joined us and his sister at our apartment for Thanksgiving dinner. I will always appreciate Cracker Barrel for the delightful Thanksgiving meal we were able to pick up there. Our son-in-law had to fly that day, so the four of us—plus Bitsy Belle—ate, napped, watched football, and relaxed as we had on so many Thanksgivings before. A comfort zone was developing, and it felt great.

Chapter 11 A New Normal

An important reason for our choosing to go to Virginia, besides wanting to be near our daughter, was access to the National Rehabilitation Hospital in Washington. A friend of Mary Margaret's volunteered to take us there for an evaluation and to schedule Ron's continued therapy, but when we got there I knew immediately that it would be our only trip to this facility. The traffic was certainly a deterrent, but worse than that, the hospital was cold and depressing. The staff was professional but lacked the warmth of the staff at Spain Rehab. Perhaps I was spoiled, but I knew this atmosphere was not what Ron needed. I knew we would never again experience the care and exceptional treatment he had received at Spain.

When we returned home, I wrote a long letter to the administrator at Spain, telling him how critically important the doctors, nurses, therapists, and support staff had been in Ron's recovery, and describing in detail many of the times they gave far more than we expected. Later we learned that the administrator put my letter in their personnel files and threw a pizza party to thank them for all they did for us.

I made an appointment for an evaluation at an outpatient therapy center about twenty minutes from our apartment. The drive there was a challenge—I knew I would have several connecting roads to learn—but our first visit told me we had found a place where Ron would improve and be safe and happy. When we arrived at the front entrance, my car was met by two uniformed valets who took the wheelchair out of the trunk and set it near Ron's door. I helped Ron into his chair and gave the keys to a valet, and we entered the front door. Everything was decorated for the holidays. There was an expansive foyer with a beautifully decorated thirty-foot Christmas tree and a player piano playing Christmas music. To our right was a circular cafeteria where visitors, patients, staff, doctors, and nurses were having lunch together. We took the elevator to the therapy floor, and when we exited we were facing a glass hallway through which we could see mountains in the distance. The hallway was also decorated for Christmas, as was the entrance to the therapy gym.

The receptionist questioned me about Ron as though he wasn't there. Because of my Spain experience, I knew this was something I did not want to recur. Ever so politely I said, "You can ask my husband. He's right here." She looked down at Ron in his wheelchair and, a bit flustered, said, "Good Morning, Mr. Ron. How are you this morning?" She chatted with us for a few minutes until the therapist arrived. Later, when Ron was out of earshot, the receptionist apologized to me for ignoring him, saying she knew better than to do that. I assured her that it was not a problem and no offense was taken. I had recognized and handled the situation as I had been taught to do by the staff at Spain, and it was resolved, just as they assured me it would be.

Ron and I loved his therapist the moment we met her. She asked Ron to take a walk with her and asked me to follow him with his wheelchair. Ron started out with his quad cane, and then she took it from him and asked him to use the railing on the hallway wall. She carried his cane as they walked and talked. After about ten feet, Ron said he was ready to sit down; she just smiled and said they were going to walk to the window at the end of the hall so they could look at the mountains in the distance. Then they would walk back. I was surprised, and I wanted to warn her that Ron would be too tired—he hadn't walked that far before. Fortunately, I did not say a word. I just followed along, and they did exactly what she said. She had stolen my heart, and I learned over lunch in that delightful cafeteria that she had stolen Ron's heart, too. If she said he could do it, he did his best to prove her right.

Our days became something of the "new normal" we had been told would occur. Three days a week I took Ron to therapy, and early each school morning I would hear a key turn in our front door lock and hear Mary Margaret call, "Puppy day care!" As I heard the door lock click again, I would see Bitsy Belle running full-speed down the hallway to our bedroom. She would leap onto our bed, full of energy and morning chill, and give us kisses. Then she would settle into bed and keep us both warm.

The Mid-Atlantic climate was a major adjustment. The breezeway to our apartment was like an artic wind tunnel that we had to traverse three days a week. Snow was quite an experience, as well. Besides learning how to dress Ron and me for the winter, learning to drive safely in winter weather was a major learning curve—and I must say I mastered it quite well.

Our dining area had bay windows, so on winter days we would sit at our table having breakfast or afternoon coffee and admire the snow-covered scenery dotted with small holly bushes that produced crimson berries. It was a peaceful landscape which we both treasured.

Over all my years as a young wife and then a mother, Christmas was my favorite time. I loved the holiness of the season, which inspired such reflection and appreciation for our many blessings. Decorating for Christmas was a month-long ritual that I anticipated from the first cold snap. I loved shopping and the excitement of wrapping gifts. Now, with our son planning to come and spend Christmas with us, the season was especially exciting for me. Our son-in-law visited with Ron, while Mary Margaret and I shopped for decorations for our little home. Buying a Christmas tree and all the trimmings was unexpectedly bittersweet for me; I couldn't help but remember all the precious ornaments I had collected over the years—the ornaments I had made with our kids and the ones they made for us were such treasures. They weren't "stuff" to me. They were yet more historical artifacts that evoked invaluable memories and documented the important people and times in our lives. Still, with Mary Margaret's help, our apartment looked like a Christmas card, and it made our family feel normal again.

The church we finally settled on was not like our cathedral back home. But it was as traditional as we could find, and it filled a void. Once again we were spending time expressing our love and appreciation for the completeness our faith provided. We had bad, *really* bad memories of our recent trials, but somehow during the Christmas season they faded, and new memories covered them like a warm blanket. At our Christmas dinner we were all together at our lovely table. It wasn't my china, silver, and crystal of thirty years—it was all new. Yet the feelings were the same.

Ron's stroke seemed to have erased the verbal "filters" we all develop through life; I had noticed how he would say things that were best left unsaid, and the psychologist who worked with us at Spain explained that this was an expected side effect of the type of stroke Ron had suffered. We had been assured he would gain more control of the distance from thought to verbal expression, and we were working on that. Midway through our Christmas dinner, Ron raised his wine glass and announced to the family that he would like to share a toast. We were delighted and raised our wine glasses. With that precious, dimpled smile, he said, "To me and your mother. We can still have sex." I had never been so embarrassed, and I'm sure our kids were as taken aback as I was. It was our son-in-law who broke the ice. He laughed and said, "Well good for you, Poppy. Good for you." Today I still chuckle at that Christmas toast. We'd never had one like it and, so far, we haven't had one like it since. I have learned that at times our new normal isn't quite normal at all.

Ron and Bitsy Belle in our apartment in Fairfax, Virginia, at Christmastime.

Chapter 12 Moving On

Throughout the winter I spent part of each day making arrangements for our return to Biloxi. I had mastered caring for Ron and had begun to look to our future. I had had our property cleared and wanted to sell it, but Ron loved it and finally convinced me he just couldn't get better until he was back on the bay. It was as if a part of him was missing, and only rebuilding on our property could give that piece back. As I drove Ron to and from therapy in Virginia, I noticed the concrete embankments that supported the highways along our route. I determined that we would build our house back, but we would build it with the stability of those concrete walls.

Only one beachfront home on Highway 90 in Pass Christian, Mississippi, had survived Katrina. It was gutted by the storm, but it maintained its structural integrity. As I studied the new building codes being determined for the coast, I searched for the person who had built that home. I learned from a friend that the homeowner was an engineer who not only built the house but was also helping develop the new federal codes. I contacted him, and soon we were planning our new home.

I bought stacks of home magazines and began tearing out pictures of what I wanted. I bought books of house plans and used them to draft hundreds of ideas. I didn't know when I would return home, but when I did return I would know what I wanted to build and who would engineer the plans. Ron and I were filled with anticipation. We had long discussions about what he wanted, and I was constantly thinking about how to make his wants happen while making our new home safe.

The highway patrol was a big part of Mississippi Special Olympics, as they conduct the torch run through the length of the state to Biloxi for the summer games. Through his longtime involvement with the event, Ron had become very close to these men. Because of this, Ron wanted to attend a fundraising event hosted by the Maryland highway patrol, which had helped in south Mississippi after Katrina. I was not in favor of this trip, even though it was only a couple of hours away. Mary Margaret and Scott insisted that they were capable of taking him to the event and that I should take that time for myself. After a little thought, I agreed. He could go, and I could sleep. Sleep had become something of a rarity for me, as Ron seldom slept longer than a couple of hours, and if he moved, I awoke. So they bundled up and went on their road trip, while I stayed in my nightclothes and slept and read most of the day. It was a wonderful treat for us both!

Ron, Mary Margaret, and Scott on a road trip.

One morning the phone rang, and I was surprised to learn that we had qualified for a FEMA trailer. The woman from FEMA explained that mobile home parks were being developed for those who had lost their homes in Katrina. When I explained that Ron was now handicapped, she replied that a wheelchair-accessible home could be provided. Finally, Ron's effort to register at FEMA—CNN reporter and cameraman in tow—had resulted in this opportunity. It had taken months, but we were thrilled. I thought that living in a neighborhood with people who had suffered the losses we had suffered would be the cathartic experience we needed.

I was surprised by my younger brother's reaction to my good news. We talked for a long while as he tried to convince me that these mobile home parks would not be as I imagined. He believed we would not be safe, would not identify with our neighbors, and would be forced to remain in the FEMA mobile home park because there were no apartments or houses to rent. His explained that the changes the coast was experiencing could be difficult for an older couple, especially when one of them was handicapped. However, when the paperwork arrived, we signed it and sent it back to FEMA. This was our chance to return home, and I was determined to take it.

My brother called with a proposition for us: we could put our mobile home on his property, since he had plenty of room, or we could put it on a small piece of property he owned about two blocks from his home. He would clear the lot and have all the necessary electrical and plumbing hookups done. I knew this meant a lot of work and expense for him. Codes and codes and more codes would have to be met; applications for the project would require city approval. I didn't want to add to his workload. Katrina had shifted his home on its foundation, and he was in the midst of having this corrected while living in a camper in his backyard. My brother and his family were very close to us. As strongly as I felt about not adding to his responsibilities, he felt just as strongly about our avoiding the mobile home park.

After many discussions with our kids, we decided to try to get the mobile home placed on the property near my brother's home. Once approvals were given, the lot was cleared and all the hookups were completed. My brother oversaw the process and sent us pictures of every step. I was so filled with anticipation that I spent hours on the telephone finding doctors, making appointments, and setting up therapy schedules for Ron. He would have pool therapy again, and he could hardly wait to get back into the water. Since few furniture stores were open on the Mississippi coast, I bought furniture for the new house I planned to build, had our rented furniture removed, and filled our apartment with the lovely new pieces I would eventually place in our new home.

Our son drove to Virginia, packed our car with essentials, drove it to the Mississippi coast, and unpacked in our mobile home. The work Michael did for us there was much like the work our daughter and son-in-law had done for us in Fairfax. He hung curtains and set up the kitchen, bedrooms, and bathroom. He then flew back to Virginia, retrieved his car, and drove back to Prattville. When we arrived on the coast later, we would find a precious little mobile home two blocks from my brother and his family. How blessed we are to have such a loving, caring family.

As it got closer to our springtime departure from Fairfax, we began to feel melancholy. One of the most treasured parts of our life there was Bitsy Belle; we had both grown so attached to her that the idea of not hosting "puppy day care" really upset us. Seeing this, our daughter set her mind to finding a maltipoo for us. We fell in love with the puppy she found. We named her Mandy, and soon our lives revolved around our little puppy-girl.

Mandy suddenly became ill, and I panicked when the veterinarian said her illness could be transferred to humans. I couldn't risk the threat to Ron's health, so Mary Margaret took Mandy back to the breeder, who agreed to give her medication and nurse her back to health. Blood tests showed it was not parvo, a potentially fatal illness, so we knew Mandy would come back to us—and she did.

A week or so before we left for Mississippi, Ron had his final appointment with his neurologist in Fairfax. We were both in really good, positive moods when we arrived. The neurologist had the reports ready for Ron's new doctor in Mississippi, and he said he needed to go over them with us. He then explained how devastatingly damaged Ron's brain was as a result of his stroke. Considering the damage, he said, Ron had recovered as much as he would be able to recover. While Ron didn't seem to comprehend the impact of his prognosis, I was heartbroken for him. I realized how difficult life would be for him, for both of us.

Driving back to our apartment, I was crying and speeding. I honestly never looked at the speedometer; I just wanted to be in our apartment and away from the doctor's visit that, for all practical purposes, had just ended our hopes for a return to the wonderful life we had lived. Suddenly a patrolman on a motorcycle was waving me over to the side of the highway.

I pulled over and reached for my license, thinking, *Why shouldn't I get a ticket? How ironic is a speeding ticket to someone who will never move faster than a snail's pace again.* I was feeling ugly and diminished, and I just wanted to give up on anything positive. The patrolman asked if I knew how fast I was driving. When I told him I thought I was keeping up with traffic, he said, "No. You were passing every car in front of you and driving twenty miles an hour over the speed limit."

He then asked why I was crying, and so I told him. I told him we had been in Fairfax for several months, living near our daughter, because we had lost our home in Katrina. I told him my husband had had a severe stroke and had been recovering at a record pace—and now his neurologist had said his progress had peaked. I told him we were returning to Mississippi and that I had hoped my husband would fully recover, but I knew in my heart he wouldn't. I told him the doctor had confirmed my fears and I just couldn't handle it all right then. I told him I probably shouldn't have been driving because I was so upset, but I would be the only one driving for the rest of our lives.

The patrolman said he had been on the force for sixteen years and had never issued a warning or let a speeder go without a ticket, but he was going to do that for the first time. Then he asked me to please drive safely to our apartment and try to compose myself, and he wished us well. I thanked him, calmed down, and drove carefully home.

Sometimes angels come on motorcycles, wearing helmets. That patrolman really made me think. It seemed that for every bit of bad news we would get, there would be someone who would show he cared and help however he could. Everywhere we turned, an angel was there to be sure we turned in the right direction.

When it was time for us to fly home, I dressed Mandy in Bitsy Belle's hand-me-downs, put her in a carrier, and presented her papers to the airline, and we all boarded our direct flight to New Orleans. Of course there were tears all around, but I had my little puppy and my healing husband, and I was returning to the family I had missed for so long. I didn't have time to be sad. I had a new house to build, and I was ready!

Chapter 13 Exhale

Michael met us at the New Orleans airport and took control of everything. When we arrived at our new home, I rolled Ron up the long ramp and into the cutest little beach bungalow ever.

Our son, Michael, setting up our FEMA mobile home.

Later that night a torrential rain came. I had always heard that mobile homes weren't very safe in storms, and I wanted to try to find a motel for the night. Michael said that he was tired, his dad was tired, and we were all going to sleep. When I awoke in the morning and went outside, I immediately envisioned the flower garden I would plant in our front yard and the fenced area I would have built for Mandy alongside our home. That morning I heard birds singing and saw a squirrel scurry up a tree, and I knew the coast was still alive. I was so happy to be home.

My mother had a cousin she often talked about whose name was Sweet. I thought that because of Mandy's sweet nature, I should rename her Sweet. No one agreed. Ron liked the Barry Manilow song *Mandy*, so Mandy she stayed. One day Ron accidentally dropped a half tablet of his muscle relaxant, and when we weren't looking, Mandy found and ate it. One minute she was prancing down the hallway; the next minute she fell down and could not seem to move. She was breathing, but her open eyes were glassy. I panicked. I called our veterinarian and was told he was in surgery. Regardless, I put Mandy on a pillow in a laundry basket and raced to his office. When the vet came out of surgery, he immediately pumped Mandy full of charcoal. It was a Friday, so she was transferred to the emergency pet hospital now located in a mobile home just off the interstate. When I saw it, I was reminded of how far the Mississippi coast had to go to become normal, but I was grateful the hospital was there at all.

At the pet hospital, the veterinarian researched Ron's medications to see which one Mandy most likely had ingested. The vet was up all night with Mandy, and I was up all night with Ron. We were so intensely frightened for her, and our hearts where heavy with the thought of losing her. I called the hospital as directed, at five o'clock the next morning. The receptionist said I could come and get Mandy, but she wouldn't tell me about her progress. I asked if she could walk or if I should bring her basket. When she said I should bring the basket, I knew I had to talk with Ron and decide what to do. We discussed putting her to sleep if she was paralyzed. I would bring her home, and we would bury her in our front yard.

When I arrived at the hospital with Mandy's basket, the receptionist asked me to have a seat. *Now the bad news,* I thought. Suddenly, from around the counter pranced my sweet little Mandy! I got down on the floor and loved on her, and she gave me sweet morning kisses. I called Ron and gave him the great news: we had our Mandy back. The doctor had been awake all night with her and was finally asleep, so the receptionist told me the details of her recovery and then remarked how sweet Mandy was. I told her I almost changed her name to Sweet because of her personality, and she suggested I rename her Sweet Mandy. A few days later, when she called to see how Mandy was recovering, the doctor asked, "How is Sweet Mandy?" I could hardly respond. Our Sweet Mandy was fine.

Since ours was a FEMA mobile home, it was subject to monthly inspections. A FEMA representative would walk through the mobile home to look for damage, check the plumbing, and so forth. One inspector commented that we were fortunate that our mobile home was located in such a nice neighborhood; in one FEMA park, a drug dealer had broken into homes, demanding monthly payments to him and his gang if the residents wanted to live. No one contacted authorities until a FEMA inspector arrived and found that an elderly couple, one of whom was handicapped, had been murdered. Our inspector said that the drug dealer and his gang had been arrested and I should watch the newspaper for details. I was so unnerved that I immediately blocked the conversation from my memory. I never searched for details. My younger brother had been so right, his strong guidance such a blessing. I will be forever grateful to him for his good advice and hard work on our behalf.

Christmas in our mobile home was quite a challenge. If we wanted to use the Christmas tree we bought in Fairfax, we had to give up a chair. And if we used the outdoor white lights we had in our holly bushes at Fairfax, the neighborhood would reach an all-time low! When you're decorating a mobile home, less is best. We bought a narrow tree that didn't overwhelm the small area, went light on decorations, and chose a small nativity set.

Michael was with us for Christmas, and during his visit he told us that he was thinking of leaving the Air Force—he thought it would be good to return home so he could help us whenever we needed him. We explained that we were fine, that soon we would be building our new house. We were confident we could convince our son that his life did not have to be intertwined in ours. Over time, however, we realized that he would be coming home.

Chapter 14 New Beginnings

One of our neighbors to the east was a retired civil service artist whom Ron knew well from his last years before retirement. She lived on the corner. Between her house and our mobile home was her daughter's house; they would be our neighbors. They were both artists, and during Katrina they had lost the gallery they owned in downtown Gulfport. Now the daughter taught art students, and they would have their painting lessons on the back porch of her house. I watched from my back stoop as the oil paintings came to life. She was a talented artist and teacher.

Eventually, I went to see this young woman and asked if she could come to our mobile home a couple of days a week to give Ron art lessons. She agreed. So three days a week Ron went to therapy, and two days a week he had art lessons. He and his teacher bonded immediately. They talked and painted together, and some days she would even stay and have lunch with us. We both grew to love her, and the works she helped Ron produce were remarkable. Yet another angel had entered our lives.

As spring approached I planted my flower garden, and soon our little front yard began to come alive. A large oak tree in the yard served as an umbrella; its shade made it a pleasure to be outdoors. But Ron couldn't share this experience with me—it was too difficult to maneuver his wheelchair in the grass. I decided he needed to enjoy the fresh air as much as I did, so I had a small screened porch built that opened to the ramp. Now Ron and I could enjoy my flower garden and have our morning coffee outdoors, as we had done so many times before Katrina. Mandy and I went for daily walks on the same sidewalks I had used to get to school as a child. I felt a sense of peace that I hadn't felt for a long time. Our walks had to be brief because I was leaving Ron alone during his nap time; we were never gone longer than fifteen minutes. Mandy so enjoyed our outings that I decided it was time to fence an outdoor area for her to enjoy whenever she liked.

Our neighbors had a little dog named Matisse. Mandy would bark hello to Matisse, and Matisse would bark hello back. It was the cutest conversation to witness! Mandy and Matisse had play days in our mobile home and became great friends. Still, Mandy needed her own space outdoors, so I approached our son with my plan. One weekend he came home from Prattville and bought lattice fencing and large fence posts. Our neighbors' homes were Victorian in style, and I felt sorry that we had parked a trailer right next to their lovely homes. Somehow I thought that a white lattice fence along our property lines would be more acceptable to the neighborhood than wood or wire. The following weekend Michael returned, and before we knew it, Mandy's outdoor territory was born. She loved it. She ran and sniffed every minute I would let her outside. She was safe and happy. Ron and I were safe and happy. And my plans for our new home had finally begun and again, our tenacity to see it to fruition would be paramount.

One day while our son was building the fence, I saw from the window that our artist friend was talking with him. Later that day they went for coffee. I mentioned their meeting at the fence to Ron, and we looked at each other and smiled. Maybe, just maybe, we were witnessing a truly new beginning. We were. A year later, they were married.

Ron and I loved being in the middle of their courtship. Occasionally they took us on double dates to movies and out to dinner. Just as we had done with our daughter and son-in-law, we shared special times with our son and Cecily, the young lady he loved. One of the most memorable was our first Mardi Gras after we returned home. Michael and his fiancé, Mary Margaret and Scott, and Ron and I returned to our condominium at the Chateau for four days of fun. Mary Margaret and I rode in the Iris parade and threw beads to the crowds all day. Michael saw to it that his dad attended the parade, and we all had a lovely dinner and later partied at Pat O'Brien's.

Our family the first time back to Mardi Gras and Pat O'Brien's.

It was wonderful to return to New Orleans as a family and experience the culture of the city as we had done for so many years. The experience proved to be exhausting for Ron, however—and somewhat so for all of us. We went to Mardi Gras for several days only one more time. Now we go for day trips, and that works fine for us. New beginnings mean a new normal.

After Mardi Gras, Michael submitted the paperwork to leave the air force. He had sustained injuries to his knee that had to be repaired, so he came home for the surgery and physical therapy. A civilian doctor would perform the surgery, and his physical therapy would be at the Air Force base in Biloxi.

So on one end of our FEMA mobile home I had Ron, and on the other end I had our son. What a nest of walking wounded we were! Michael had been so good to us through Katrina, Ron's stroke, and all our relocations; it was an honor to care for him during his recuperation. As a mom, I loved having him with us so I could care for him. Michael came through his surgery and therapy fine. He rented out his home in Prattville and moved in with us. I cannot say what a help he was. With Michael there, I was able to go visit family or have my hair and nails done without rushing or worrying about Ron. Most important, I was able to return to teaching a course at the university in the fall. I felt like my old self, and it felt good.

That summer our daughter and Bitsy Belle came and stayed a whole month with us. The little living room now housed a bed that we could set up and take down with ease. Mary Margaret was very unhappy at how our lives had changed. She wanted to be near us and to help me. We talked about how difficult it would be for us to visit her as we had before Katrina and Ron's stroke. This was a reality that we could not change. As Ron's full-time caregiver, I couldn't travel without him. And traveling was hard on Ron. We would have to accept our distance and live within its confines.

But Mary Margaret would not accept this new normal. She began to insist that Scott relocate her to the Mississippi coast and commute to be with her. Over time, his resistance and her insistence became a battle that was not good for either of them or their marriage. I felt trouble brewing, but I could not seem to help prevent it.

Both of our children, it seemed, needed to sacrifice for us. I was unsettled about this and didn't know how to handle it. I loved them both and wanted them to be happy, and I could see that they were considering or making life-changing decisions, possibly negative ones, because of us. I worried about them and felt guilty that Ron and I had such strife at our age, and I feared that it would affect the children we had tried so hard to raise without conflict. Ron's therapy was going well, and his outlook was so improved that I felt I shouldn't share my concerns with him; I knew he would have to use a quad cane and wheelchair for the rest of his life, and that was burden enough. So I protected him from any upset that I could. I didn't want him to realize that Katrina was still destroying plans and goals and forcing undesirable choices. I prayed about my concerns for our children and put them in God's hands, as I had so many times before.

Chapter 15 Making Memories

Every Fourth of July for many years, my older brother hosted his family, extended family, and friends for a party at his home on Highway 90, just across from the beach. We loved having daylong visits on his long front porch, taking the kids to the beach, setting off fireworks, eating traditional Lebanese food made from recipes passed down by our father, and splurging on our sister-in-law's homemade ice cream.

After my brother and his family lost their home down to the slab in Katrina, they relocated to a small cabin they owned on a large piece of property with a big pond. They were rebuilding, too, so whenever they were in town they would stop by our mobile home, where we would have optimistic conversations about our new home plans and about building codes and contractors and such. As the Fourth of July approached, we decided we would gather at our mobile home for a small party. We celebrated the day with hot dogs and banana splits, and then we went to see the fireworks on the beach that evening. Mary Margaret was home with us, Michael was home with us, and we were surrounded by loved ones, laughter, and great expectations. Even Mandy had her cousin, Bitsy Belle, to enjoy for the holiday.

*Ron and some family members enjoying our Fourth
of July in our FEMA mobile home.*

After the holiday, Mary Margaret and Bitsy Belle returned to
Virginia. We all missed them. Mandy particularly missed Bitsy Belle;
she would look for her friend and wait at the door for her for hours.
I began to search the newspapers for a maltipoo to be Mandy's sister
and playmate. When I found an advertisement for maltipoo puppies,
my niece and I drove to Mobile to see them, leaving my younger
brother at home to keep Ron company. I found Sissy, who at three
months was a bit older than typical puppies for sale. She had been
overlooked when the rest of her siblings had been purchased. She
had a unique yellowish coat, and her beautiful little face looked a bit
more maltese than Mandy's, so I knew I could tell them apart. Sissy
slept in my niece's lap, her face in the crook of my niece's elbow, all
the way home.

Our first priority was a bath. We were told Sissy had ear mites, which
the breeder had treated with a powder that Sissy hated. In fact, Sissy
would not come to the breeder and spent most of her time outdoors;
her plight was one of the reasons I chose her. To our amazement, when
Sissy was bathed, we found she had a beautiful bright-white coat. What
I was able to clean from her ears repulses me still.

Her visit to our veterinarian was very successful. She was healthy once she healed from being spayed, and she became the perfect companion for Mandy. They played day and night, indoors and out. They rolled and wrestled, and nipped and chased each other. We had constant entertainment. Ron absolutely loved our puppy dogs, and we love them even more now.

Mandy and Sissy in our FEMA mobile home.

Meanwhile, our awesome engineer had completed the structural plans for our new home. They were designed like a beachfront condominium. The home's foundation would begin with twelve thirty-five-foot treated poles pounded into the bedrock. Above that would be spiral rebar and a concrete perimeter foundation. Then we would have a chain wall with fill, and a slab on which to build our house. The house was engineered with an unbroken connection from bedrock to rooftop. Its walls would consist of eight inches of solid concrete with rebar reinforcement. Our new home would not succumb to Mother Nature if we could possibly prevent it.

The planning and building process required us to spend a good amount of time at the property, about thirty minutes away from our mobile home. This quickly became impossible. I couldn't leave Ron for such a long time, and he couldn't go with me due to the outdoor heat. So I sought a rental house near our property. After a few weeks, to my amazement, the perfect house just down the street from our property had a "For Rent" sign in its yard. I called the owner, toured the house, and signed a lease that day. The sign was in the yard for only one day.

The move meant we had to buy yet more furniture, as the furniture for our new house was in storage and the FEMA furniture had to remain in the mobile home. Once the new furniture was delivered, movers packed our mobile home accessories and we bid farewell to our neighborhood. I would miss walking to my brother's house and seeing him and his family frequently. And I would really miss the homemade dinners my sister-in-law liked to drop off at our door.

My older brother had a high school friend who told him about a contractor who built concrete houses at a good price. If I chose this contractor, construction would be considerably less than I had expected to pay. So when the foundation was complete, I handed the plans over to this new contractor, anticipating that we'd be in our new home in about six months. He started out well, but then he needed more money and less was getting accomplished. After several unpleasant conversations, I drove to his office to either get some firm completion dates or end the contract.

When I reached his office, there was a note taped to the door saying that the contractor had left the area. An attorney's business card was attached as a contact. What followed was terribly predictable. Many people on the coast had contracted with fly-by-night contractors who left them broke and homeless. I feared we might be in that group, and we were.

Fortunately, our new rental was just perfect for us. I had a study once again, and the puppy dogs had a big, fenced backyard. Ron and I could enjoy our coffee on a covered patio, and the home's wood floors made it easier for Ron to walk. To make life even more comfortable for him, we installed rails in the bathroom and purchased a motorized wheelchair. Now Ron had new freedom.

Convenience was the new state of affairs. Our rental house was two minutes from the construction site, so I could be on site or at home with Ron quickly. Ron's water therapy was nearby, too. We really enjoyed the year and a half we lived in the rental.

During this time, Ron and I were delighted to hear that Michael and Cecily had become engaged and were planning a Christmastime wedding. How perfect was this! Our rental house would be perfect for entertaining, I could use both Christmas trees and all the decorations

I wanted. Our home would be festive for the pre-wedding parties and visitors. We could celebrate in many of the ways we did before Katrina.

The wedding couldn't have been lovelier. After the newlyweds returned from their Antigua honeymoon, we hosted a New Year's Eve party for our family and our work crew. It wasn't too cool for the party to spill onto the patio, so there was plenty of space. We had always hosted New Year's celebrations in our home, so continuing this tradition was very special for us. We knew it would be a good year we were ringing in, and our hearts were light. We were making new memories and creating a new life.

Chapter 16 Tenacity Rules

After having been so disappointed and exploited by our contractor, I decided to be the new contractor for our home. I filed all the paperwork, studied the codes closely, and hired the framers who were already involved with our home, as they understood the engineering and house plans. Framing progressed while I sought subcontractors for the flooring, lighting, air conditioning, wrought iron, tile, appliances, cabinets, millwork, swimming pool, and so many other things.

The federal, state, county, and city codes aligned fairly well. If I was careful and relied on the Biloxi code office, which I did, I could meet all of them. The house had to be twenty-five feet above sea level. The first level could not be a living area, and water had to be free to flow through that floor at will. Our first level now houses a garage, a stairway, an elevator, a pool room, and a heated therapy pool for Ron. Large windows at the front of the house, a lovely iron door with windows that open, and open grates every few feet around the bottom of the walls would allow floodwater—something we hoped would never come—to flow freely through the bottom of the structure. A four-foot-high, solid concrete wall, built like the exterior walls of the house, serves as a seawall separating the marsh area from our home. That wall contains a flower garden that meets the back of the house. The first level of our house is another four feet above and borders the garden.

The second level is where Ron and I live most of the time. It includes a study, a kitchen with a two-sided fireplace whose other side is in the living room, a dining area, a master suite with closets, a bath with a shower and hot tub, and a laundry room. There is a second bath near the winding stairway to the third level. The third level has a living room and two bedroom suites, and a partial fourth level is bay-shaped. I call it a loft; Ron calls it "the lighthouse." For many years he had wanted to build a lighthouse on Lopez Point, and now the bay side of our house resembles one. Ron is very pleased.

The back of the house is mostly windows on every level except the first, which has open arches. The windows on the bay side and the sides of the house have hurricane shutters that sustain winds of 150 mph, while the front of the house has handmade wooden shutters that are decorative and strong. There are balconies and large white columns on the second and third levels.

All the floors in our new home are wood except the kitchen, baths, and ground floor, which are tile; the smooth surfaces are easy for Ron to navigate.

Ron loves our home. We have a pier that goes out to the dock, and he goes there on his Jazzy and watches the birds and boaters. We also have a large pavilion where we have family cookouts and shrimp boils when the weather is pleasant.

Building the new house took two years, a lot of money, and constant problem solving. But the investment was worth it. When we moved in, we enjoyed just sitting in each new room, getting to know it. Now we both feel as if we are finally home.

The street view of our new home.

The bay side of our new home.

Shortly after we moved into our new home, Mary Margaret told us she felt so unhappy and alone that she had decided to file for divorce and return to the coast to be with family. For most of their ten-year marriage, Scott had been away from home, flying—a way of life she had accepted and to which she had adjusted. Before Katrina, before Ron's strokes, their marriage had been relatively uneventful and happy. Now everything had changed for our daughter. Life was uncertain, and being alone so often with just her work and friends no longer filled her need to be connected. She wanted to be where she could help us and be a part of whatever life Ron and I would share. She wanted to be near her brother and his new wife. She wanted her family.

Scott would not transfer from Washington DC to a new base in Chicago or Denver and then travel on his days off to be with her here on the coast. He knew their marriage would not work if they had to schedule visits to see each other, and if he had to live in temporary quarters when he wasn't here with her. He loved his boat and being on the water, something he couldn't enjoy in Chicago or Denver. They simply could no longer meet one another's needs, and Mary Margaret chose to come back home.

We loved Scott and were very upset that their marriage was ending. He was hoping that if Mary Margaret spent more time at home with us, her demands would change and they could come to an agreement that would prevent the divorce. Our daughter did not see the situation as he did. By summer she was divorced, had bought a home five minutes from ours, had found a teaching position, and was not looking back. I knew this dramatic change would take a toll on her at some point, and I felt guilty that our misfortune had resulted in such upheaval in her life. We are still sorry and sad that her marriage ended, and we hope she will find happiness here.

After a year of proving to herself she could be self-reliant and independent, Mary Margaret rented her house and moved into our home. She has a demanding career as her school's instructional coach, a boyfriend we like and respect, and as much of a social life as she wants. Our daughter is such a help and a joy to us; we can never reward her enough for her love and for sharing her life with us. Bittersweet defines this new normal.

With our daughter's return home, Bitsy Belle once again became part of our household, and now she has a brother! Mary Margaret and I went to the Fairhope Art Festival in Alabama and came home with some lovely artwork—and a Corgi mix named Jack. When we found him, he was in a shelter and only a week from leaving this world. Even if we hadn't known that, we would have brought Jack home with us. He has a long body and short, stocky legs, and his fur is the color of the Saints logo—golden, black, and white. His markings are beautiful, and he is the most kind-hearted, loving, precious little grandson dog we could want.

And in case you're counting—yes, we now have four dogs and our daughter living with us. There is plenty of room for more, but right now we have enough. Our lives are filled with entertainment!

Chapter 17 The Water Lies

After depositions, engineering reports, and every delay tactic the insurance company could think of, we were awarded damages from our wind insurance. It took years of follow-up and substantial legal fees, but we finally have a sense of satisfaction that we got what we paid for. The contractor who walked out with our savings and our confidence is in prison, thanks to Mississippi Attorney General Jim Hood and the department charged with investigating Katrina fraud.

I'm sorry to say that the wonderful construction company that framed our house is out of business. One of its owners, a brilliant, creative, and reliable man, was killed in a motorcycle accident. His young life is gone, and with it his talent and skill. All the other crew members moved away, and I no longer hear from them. Yet when I am in the loft writing, or in the pool guiding Ron's therapy, or just admiring the beauty and strength of our home, I think of them and smile. Building this home was a bigger accomplishment than my career in education, bigger than earning four degrees including a doctorate, and bigger than everything in between, except raising our children. It took a tenacity I didn't know I had, consistent, knowledgeable help from the Biloxi code offices, and talented workers who performed with the utmost care and professionalism. As Ron often tells me, "This is a beautiful home you built for me. It is a big deal." It was certainly a big deal for me!

Every time I see Ron struggle to walk with the weight of his paralyzed side, I wish I could do more for him. He has such a hill to climb every day, and there is little I can do to make his climb easier. He has the sweetest, most pleasant attitude; we are so blessed that he isn't bitter or resentful. He appreciates every little thing anyone does for him. He loves being home on the water again, and I'm happy, too—yet I'll always have a nagging feeling that we are not safe here.

We've spared nothing to prevent another catastrophe, and in that spirit I equipped the new house with an uninterrupted power system. But I will never again hear the unrelenting, determined, furious wind I heard in Katrina. I will never again see the calm, beautiful bay we love turn angry, violent, and destructive. I will never again fear for our lives because of a storm. If another hurricane threatens our coastline, we will not be here.

I have often thought of the large oil painting I bid on and bought at the Special Olympics auction just before Katrina. It was titled *The Water Never Lies*. But it does. I have learned that the calm and beauty we see is merely a façade for what the water can become. Its calm is deceptive; the water cannot be trusted. It performs for Mother Nature: she rules, and the water obeys. Yes, the water lies.

Even knowing this, we are blessed and happy to see the water every day. The image of an orange sun going down in the west, setting the water ablaze, is breathtaking. The light of a full moon sparkling on the water is a sight to behold. Boaters enjoying the water and the island just behind us afford us such entertainment; watching and hearing the tugboats as they bring the coal barges upriver to the power plant evokes such nostalgia. Because of the water, our backyard neighbors are lovely birds and a beautiful, untouched marsh. Sitting on the dock, listening to the waves break as a boat passes, watching the fish jump, and pulling up crab baskets, the blue crabs inside clicking and clacking their claws, are experiences only the water can provide. These are experiences we love and appreciate.

The water is like the little girl in the nursery rhyme: "When she was good, she was very, very good; but when she was bad, she was horrid." We love that little girl and always will, yet we clearly, deeply acknowledge the terrible things of which she is capable.

We have established our new normal. It hardly reflects our life before Katrina, but we are alive and somewhat content, and we recognize how blessed we are. The strength of our family, the will of our community, and the love and commitment we have for each other fill our lives and give us hope that our future will be one without hills too steep for us to climb.

We are one family sharing one story of the impact of Hurricane Katrina. There are thousands and thousands of families with stories that will never be shared—stories that may well be more profound and compelling than ours. We sense their experiences and embrace them, gathering strength and tenacity from all their trials and their will to overcome. From all those untold stories we gain a special understanding that bonds us to their tragedies and their successes; we are among a unique people who have experienced what most others have not. The experience makes us more thoughtful, more prudent, more aware, more understanding, and more compassionate. The strangers who have faced adversity and stood tall are a part of us, and their untold stories are a part of our stories, a part of our very being. Because we are not alone in our experience, we can never go back to who we were. We are older and wiser now, and grateful for the opportunity to grow in the wisdom this new normal offers us.

Acknowledgments

Before I express my appreciation for those who have had a positive impact on our lives, I want to share my perspective on natural disasters. In particular, I want to acknowledge a perspective that seems to be ignored when we consider the victims of these disasters.

As I write this portion of my book, Hurricane Irene is traveling through the Mid-Atlantic and Northeast. I am listening to the Weather Channel, ABC News, and CNN, and I've noticed that they all report the news in a common manner. Reporters speak to mayors, and mayors speak to and of first responders. We hear how everyone is concerned about flooding and downed trees, and how they have tried to help the elderly and people in hospitals to ensure their safety. They mention other storms, including Katrina. What they don't clarify is that the statistics, the level of the hurricane winds and storm surge, the precautions and the preparations, are measurements and actions that constitute part of the emergency plan. The people, the lives that are being impacted, are the part of the story they don't know and can't share.

People who survive a natural disaster will see their lives change in unpredictable ways. They are not invisible factors in emergency plans. They are not statistics. They are flesh and blood. They have hopes and dreams. They have histories of hard work, failures, and successes. They are the elemental parts of families and communities, cultures and traditions that will never be the same. They will feel fear that cannot be ignored or forgotten once it is experienced, and their bodies will continue to react to that fear long after the initial disaster has played itself out. In many ways they will never be whole. Only the name of the storm and the financial costs will be remembered. The people who live through the rage of natural disasters become an afterthought. As one of them, I want to acknowledge them. I want to say I am so sorry for your trauma and your losses. I am so moved by your resilience to start over in your new life, and by your strength to put your past in a place where it can be respected and remembered. I want to acknowledge how it feels to have a broken heart and a broken spirit, and how difficult it is to overcome all the obstacles a natural disaster produces.

Most of all, I want to recognize the importance of healing and recovery and hope and faith. I know those of you who survived a disaster met the stress, upset, and cruelty it brought. I also know you met angels who stepped into your life at just the right moment, bringing peace, calm, and goodness.

This is the message the media cannot deliver. They can tell you how to prepare for the disaster, but they cannot tell you how to pack your emergency kit with angels. God packs that kit for you, and He delivers it when you need it. Angels are more necessary than stockpiling water and food, boarding your windows, or evacuating. Once you've done those things, the angels come and help you rebuild your life. You can count on them, and you will recognize them for the comfort they bring.

There are so many people who have helped us in any way they could. The initial, most critical help came from our children, who stepped up immediately and shouldered as much responsibility as we would allow. I am so very proud of them. Mary Margaret and Michael are young people who love their parents and care as much about our well-being as they care about their own—if not more. We thank God for the adults they have become, and we will be forever grateful for their influence in our lives.

The neighbors whose home was our safe harbor were critically important in saving our lives. I can't express how blessed we were that they were home and welcomed us. We don't discuss our Katrina experience with them; it's better for all of us to look ahead. But I am certain they know how much we love and appreciate them.

My nieces who found and secured us after the storm may never know the positive impact of their actions. My niece who handled Ron's transfer from Pascagoula to Spain Rehab is so bright and capable; our lives made an upturn as a result of her efforts.

Receiving good health care was critical to Ron's survival and recovery. With our area totally devastated, doctors, nurses, and other medical personnel left their own homes and families to help those of us who desperately needed them. It must have been torturous for them to relocate their families, or leave them each day, and come to the hospital to repair the health and lives of strangers. They eased our suffering and replenished our spirits.

We so needed the friends and family who came to visit with us in our "living room" in the Pascagoula hospital's radiology clinic. The feeling that we were still valued by and connected to them gave us hope. Those who took the time and effort to see us in Birmingham will always be special. They gave us a reason to be strong as we anticipated their visits with excitement.

My friend and colleague from the university didn't just offer me her home—she also offered her love and her spirit of hope. I will be forever grateful to her.

Our son's friends who brought us a travel trailer and made us homemade treats, and others who gave me clothes, purses, and encouragement, should know they were instrumental in our will to overcome our tragedy and move ahead with confidence.

No words can describe how much respect and appreciation we have for the medical staff at Spain Rehab. No amount of money can repay them for the profound difference they made in our lives. They are dedicated angels who share and monitor and support and encourage. Each of them is bright and capable. They give life to humbled, hurt, helpless people. They are miracle workers who worked miracles in our lives. God bless Spain Rehab Center at UAB.

Ron's doctors and therapists in Virginia will always be special to us, as will be the water therapist here in Biloxi. They gave us the skills to determine our future.

Last but certainly not least, I offer a heartfelt acknowledgement of the people of the Mississippi coast. Calling them "survivors" doesn't do them justice. These people are re-creating the familiar place they loved from a devastated world. Too few have returned to the coastline, but many have returned and settled a little north of there. Yes, they returned. They lived in camper trailers and mobile homes until they could rebuild their homes. They met in church tents until they could rebuild their churches. They rebuilt their businesses, schools, highways, and bridges. They reestablished their communities and rebuilt historic sites, museums, parks, and playgrounds. They rebuilt and reopened their harbors and their port. They reached out for help, and when it came, they shared it.

Even now, in 2011, the Mississippi coast is comparatively barren. Few homes have been built. Few gas stations, restaurants, or entertainment spots dot the coastline. High insurance rates have prohibited progress there. Yet the shrimp boats are working, the tourists are visiting, and the natural beauty of the area has returned. The resilience of the people who share a love of the Mississippi coast, its culture, and its quality of life is remarkable and enduring. We are proud and grateful to belong to the Mississippi Gulf Coast and be a part of these special people as we rebuild our lives together.

www.ingramcontent.com/pod-product-compliance
Lightning Source LLC
Chambersburg PA
CBHW051439280526
45785CB00003B/1346